GRACE

FOR THE

UNDESERVING

GRACE

FOR THE

UNDESERVING

DON UHM

REDEMPTION
PRESS

Originally published as *The Signs and Involvements of God,* WinePress Publishing, 2009.

Published by Redemption Press, PO Box 427, Enumclaw, WA 98022. Toll Free (844) 2REDEEM (273-3336)

Redemption Press is honored to present this title in partnership with the author. The views expressed or implied in this work are those of the author. Redemption Press provides our imprint seal representing design excellence, creative content and high quality production.

ISBN 13: 978-1-68314-109-9 (Print)

Library of Congress Catalog Card Number: 2016949625

Table of Contents

Dedication and Acknowledgments

I DEDICATE THIS book to my Lord, Jesus Christ.

A number of people contributed to my preparation of this book in various ways by stimulating my thinking with their ideas and information.

I particularly want to thank my wife, Mary, for her faithful prayers and encouragement.

Thanks, also, to my daughter, Dr. Grace Park, for her helpful review of this manuscript as it was being developed.

Thank you to my church members for their prayers, especially Terry and Tom Lee, and Dr. Edgar and Jina Flores.

For helping to birth this book, thank you to Inger Logelin for directing the editorial process, and Hannah McKenzie and Amber Payne for turning the manuscript into a book.

Preface

AT THE BEGINNING of the twenty-first century, a technologically-advanced era, our lifestyles and ways of thinking have seen great change. Rapid change and constant progress may not be easy for us to understand or accept, and may cause us to lose our direction. Local and global leaders proclaim a groundless enthusiasm for man's glorious future on earth. We only have to recall the past horrors of the wars through the twentieth and twenty-first centuries, and the unspeakable cruelties taking place today, to know human beings cannot be assured of better and better outcomes. As a result, many are filled with confusion and worry.

Can we prevent impending chaos? History shows us we cannot. Instead of finding the cause of ongoing problems, many talk positively. The illusion that the earth is of man, by man, and for man and his glory is a deception that is throwing a dark shadow on us.

Is there any hope? Can society's misery and tragic problems be healed?

In order to find an answer for the future, we must see how the universe and life began. We cannot exactly know the origin of everything, because no one can see his origin. To trace back to the origin of everything, we investigate existing nature and the life on the one hand, and other sources and records on the other hand.

The Bible is the only convincing source about the origin of the universe and life created by God, His purpose of creation, and what caused evil. To see an accurate explanation of world history from God's eternal standpoint, we will look at the earthly events that are in progression to God's final plan.

Introduction:
What to Know and Believe
and How to Live

THE WORD *LIFE* resonates with great meaning beyond our capability to fully understand it. Our optimistic mindsets cause us to search for fulfillment in our lives. But, the reality is, life is a source of unexpected adversity and problems.

We humans were appointed to live on earth in a set boundary, and were designed to interact with our Creator. Just as the design of the earth's rotation and revolution has not changed since its inception, so our lives were designed to live within appointed boundaries. We can live a maximized life only within the appointed boundaries and regulations and by complying with its system. This is the destiny of human beings. We need to know what we must do, and not do, and how to live life in relation to this truth.

Everything we do leads us inevitably to an encounter with the originator of everything, our Creator. It is our obligation to come under God's authority. To deny this is rebellion. To accept His authority allows us to experience Him for who He is. We can then live out true love, good morals, peace, and hope within God's appointed boundaries, and overcome the power of the enemy.

The will and truth of the Creator cannot be destroyed. Coming against Him only results in tragic failure and a meaningless life. When we come to the Creator, we will be back in the right position as His creatures, and we will receive true peace, unlike the world's dried-up and thirsty peace.

The Bible teaches that God created space, time, and life, as well as matter and energy. Everything God created has a systematic order. The biblical view of creation stands up when compared to other historical and archaeological records. We must not fear the patched-together findings of evolutionists and the claims of atheists. The basis of this book is rooted in the belief that God is the source of the creation of the universe and life. We will examine evidences of origins to prove their truth and reliability and learn our subsequent human responsibility.

Chapter One

A Wonderful and Intelligent Designer

The Signs and Involvements of God

AS LONG AS people have existed, their curiosity, an aspect of their ability to think and to question, has driven them to search out both their own origins and origins of other things. How did all things come to be what they are today? Are they by-products of accidental chance, or created by a super-intelligent Creator, who is self-existent?

Creationists have the simple and clear answer. It is documented in the Bible, which describes God as the Creator, who made everything "out of nothing." The existence of all things, living and non-living, and above all, mankind, remains the best historical record of evidence for creationism. Our belief in creation enables us to see the universe and life forms as dependent upon God's sustaining power, wisdom, and activity.

We are not the end products of meaningless processes in an impersonal world, but we are created in the image of a personal, loving God. God created us to be loved and He commissioned us to take dominion over the world as His earthly agents (Gen. 1:28). Knowing this, we can understand history is a way of explaining the progression of God's plan through humanity toward an ultimate destination. On this basis, we must assume the starting point of history began with the creative act of our Creator. Arthur F. Glasser says, "History means movement."[1] We must look beneath the surface of external events to find the significant meaning. History is a progressive movement toward the Creator's ultimate destination, not accidental movement without any goal.

Accordingly, history gives us the final direction of the will of God through His continuing involvement in the world. Howard A. Snyder says history is not "haphazard happenstance" and has an "external" as well as "internal" meaning.[2] James W. Sire explains, "History is linear, a meaningful sequence of events leading to the fulfillment of God's purpose for humanity, and history itself is a form of revelation and is the record of the involvement and concern of God in human events (especially as localized in the Jewish people)."[3] Paul the apostle declared the invisible connection between the historical, factual basis of God's involvement in our world and the Christian faith. "But if it is preached that Christ has been raised from the dead, how can some of you say that there is no resurrection of the dead? . . . And if Christ has not been raised, our preaching is useless and so is your faith" (1 Cor. 15:12, 14).

History reveals the signs and involvements of God through Jesus Christ. The birth, substitutional death, and resurrection of Jesus Christ, which took place in space and time, provide Christians with an absolute foundation of faith. The disciples as eyewitnesses were primary sources of these events. God sustains the world throughout time and space. He is not only Lord over the whole of history, but He continues to govern and rule in the affairs of man, based upon His eternal plan and will. John Bright, a theologian and author, says, "History must have future, a destination."[4] History began with His purposeful creation. God moves in a meaningful process toward His final stage in His dealings with creation.

The Awe and Wonder

The earth with its thin skin of rich soil, water, mountains, trees, flowers, and all kinds of precious things is a large and beautiful home for human life and all the other living creatures. When we gaze at the clear night sky after rain sweeps dusty and polluted air away, countless stars cause us to raise profound questions about the origin of the universe—especially the motions of the planets in the solar system that revolve around the sun in elliptical orbits. How and why do they make those motions without mistake? I definitely believe what scientists say: There must be complex rules or laws governing the world. Those rules have been working without stopping since it came into existence.

We breathe in oxygen and let out carbon dioxide. It is theoretically feasible that carbon dioxide could fill up the earth so no one could survive. But mankind has never run out of oxygen because cycles keep the earth's ecosystems in balance. We are surrounded by well-prepared, well-working systems in beautiful symmetry. Where and how did all of this come from? And what is the meaning of it all? In order for us to get the right answers, we need to know the definition of the word *system*.

A system is defined as group of independent but interrelated elements that make up a unified and consistent whole. By definition, if the components of a system are divided, or working against one another, they are not part of a system at all. The systems of the universe, or the order of things, have meaning and purpose and are not random. We know this to be true. For example, in order to clean dirty clothes, man invented the washing machine. The machine is equipped with many options, including settings for soil levels, fabric type, and the load size. Even though the machine has many options, they all work together to produce clean clothes.

Even man himself is a type of a system. We have a brain, heart, lungs, kidneys, nerves, hands, feet, bones, and muscles, all part of our biological makeup, or system. All of us have profound connections to this planet. All the matter around us is related for a specific purpose. Trees need dirt, wind, nutrition, water, sunlight, oxygen, and nitrogen for survival.

The rules of systems are known and proven. Professor and author Howard A. Snyder says, "All things are connected, not only by the human mind, but also more deeply, through an inbuilt or inherent order that is really there."[5] Neil Broom, a chemical and materials engineering professor, gives us an example of the existence of systems and rules. "The living cell operates in principle just like any man-made mechanical system with all the appearances of having been constructed according to principles of engineering design."[6] Systems have a well-organized order that allows us to live peacefully.

Order is defined as a maintaining factor, coherent pattern, and expression of profound natural law in the system. Its function is a connective and directive faculty within system networks toward a certain goal. Every system, therefore, functions properly. But their existence and function is mysterious from a scientific perspective. Order makes systems work normally, and systems work simultaneously with order. If you don't have order, you don't have a system, and if you don't have system you don't have order. They cannot be absolutely separable. When we have order, we find beauty, wonder, and harmony. William Demski, a mathematician and philosopher, says: "For nature to be an object of inquiry for the scientists, nature must have an order which the scientist can grasp. If nature were totally without form and order, no science would be possible."[7] We see this order everywhere, from social, political, biological, cosmological, and ecological systems, to our human bodies. We see it every time the earth revolves around the sun.

Howard Snyder says, "We see then that the universe, at least as a physical place, is marked by both order and surprise."[8] The existence of order in the various systems of the universe leads to the question of how and where this purposeful order came from. Does this order come from "accidental chance"? Is it even possible for order to create and sustain itself? We don't believe that automobiles, airplanes, cell phones, navigation devices, satellites, or any other form of technology is self-creating or self-sustaining.

They require creation and a built-in process to work properly toward a certain goal.

Why is it any different with the universe? The complexity of order in the universe points to a Creator who made all things (Gen. 1:1-31; Eccl. 3:1-8; 2 Kings 20:1; Ps. 94:9, 104:2-9; Job 9:6-12, 14:5, 26:7, 10, 38:4-7) and holds all things together (Ps. 136:5, 148:3-5). The universe and all living things must have systems of a remarkably precise order and condition, providing proper and necessary components, constants and precision, and a higher level of process and control.

Cosmology and biology give us more details.

The Cosmos

Cosmology is the study of the harmoniously and systematically well-organized physical universe, the solar system, galaxy, etc., and its origin, structure, and development. Webster's dictionary defines it as the totality of all things that exist.[9] The universe consists of a multiplicity of objects and complex systems. Paul Davis, a mathematical physicist, defines the universe as undeniably complex, but says its complexity is of an organized variety.[10] In order for people and other organisms to live, well-organized and interrelated conditions with the right elements must exist. For a harmonious balance in the universe, there must be numerous natural laws in action. Scientists discover additional natural laws on a regular basis. Physicist Hugh Ross says, "Everything about the universe tends toward man, toward making life possible and sustaining it."[11]

Here are some strong supporting evidences of a well-ordered creation:

- Stars have good balance in the force of gravity between them that allows for their harmonious stability.
- The distance between the stars leads to the stability of orbits.[12]
- This distance between the sun and the earth allows for stability for living organisms on earth.
- The earth constantly revolves around the sun, which is conducive for desirable temperatures and the changes of the seasons.
- The earth's rotation leads to the change of day and night.
- The earth is tipped at 23.5 degrees with respect to the plane of revolution around the sun, which leads to climates that are conducive for human existence.
- Planets continually rotate around the sun.
- There is constant proper gravitational interaction with the moon that allows for an effective earthly ocean tide.
- The necessary oxygen quantity in the earth's atmosphere is sufficient for living organisms.
- There are constant rainy seasons on earth that benefit all kinds of life.
- The earth consists of necessary gas levels such as oxygen, nitrogen, hydrogen, carbon dioxide, and ozone for humans and other living organisms.

Our Human Bodies

Our bodies consist of many different organs that are interrelated and interdependent, all of which make up a highly complex system.

Geoffrey Simmons, M.D., says, "The formation of each cell and every function thereof follows as a blueprint that is drawn up at the union of the egg and sperm."[13] Cell systems must be programmed by design. Consider the way the body continually goes through the process of renewal, recycle, protection, and adjustment.

The Digestive System

Food flows down the gastrointestinal tract and is absorbed through the walls of the small intestine, into the bloodstream, through the liver, extracting nutrients from food and delivering them to every cell in the body, thereby maintaining the health of the whole body.

The Immune System

White blood cells and antibodies circulate in the blood, and the antigen-antibody reaction forms immunity when harmful foreign substances such as viruses, bacterium, funguses, or parasites, invade the body. When we get sick, the produced antibody may either destroy the antigen directly or white cells can swallow up the foreign intruder by a built-in defense mechanism.

The Breathing System

When we run or go up into high altitudes, we cannot breathe normally because physiological changes take place in our bodies. After our panting mechanism kicks in to make adjustments, we eventually return to a normal breathing pattern and adjust to the new situation or climate.

The Skin System

Our skin is an organ designed to protect us. Geoffrey Simmons says our skin is the largest and heaviest organ. It weighs six to ten pounds; in the average adult it covers an area of twenty-two square feet.[14] Our skin is a highly complex system that covers the entire body with lots of functioning factors including flexes, folds, and crinkles around joints. It has varying textures like hardness, softness, and roughness. It also recognizes information about our environment, monitors the variety of stimuli in wind, and changes in pressure and temperature. Paul Brand says the "skin's most crucial contribution might opt for waterproofing."[15] Sixty percent of the body consists of fluids, and these would soon evaporate without the moist, sheltered world provided by skin. Without skin, a warm bath would kill; fluids would rush in like water over a flooded spillway, swelling the body with liquid, diluting the blood, and waterlogging the lungs. The skin's tight barrier of shingled cells fends off such disasters.[16] Skin is thickest when we need more protection. Despite the constant turnover of cells and sloughing of skin, everyone's exterior remains the same.[17]

The Muscular System

Our muscles are remarkable organs. We have more than one hundred different muscle groups.[18] They help us move, change shape, and lift heavy objects. Some muscles contribute to hand movements, and some, barely an inch long, allow for a spectrum of subtle expression in the face. The diaphragm controls coughing, breathing, sneezing, and laughing, and thigh muscles equip the body for a lifetime of walking. Without muscles, bones would collapse in a heap, joints would slip apart, and movement would cease.[19] Our muscle systems are also interrelated and work interdependently with all kinds of other organs, such as nerves, skin, arteries, and veins for harmonious motion and desirable health.

Summary

How could all these systems, so beautifully and wonderfully knit together, be accidental? Well-organized systems require a higher level of precise process and design by a designer. An accidental chance cannot survive. There is no doubt these systems are from the Creator. Modern science impacts our understanding of the Creator God in a number of ways. The constant rotation and revolution of the earth are based on accurate and orderly laws of nature.

Werner Gitt says, "Laws of nature describe events, phenomena, and occurrences which consistently and repeatedly take place. They are universally valid laws.[20] Danny R. Faulkner says, "Science would not be possible if the universe did not exhibit order and follow rules."[21] These laws of nature require an accurate design and a Designer beyond our imagination. In order for us to know the existence of God and His creation of the universe and life, we must trace back the created materials as fingerprints, because no one was present during the Designer's creation of life.

While we cannot see Him directly, we see His presence in the created world. We cannot see the wind physically, but we can see trees blown by the wind, and we feel and know the wind is real and powerful. The effects of the wind absolutely confirm the existence of the wind. No one thinks the effects of the wind are accidental. Similarly, the after effects of God in action are seen and recognized as real evidence, proving God created the universe and life with a purpose. He sustains the world throughout time and space.

In the belief of God's existence and creation we discover God's plans and purposes for us. Just as man has his purpose in his life on earth, so God has His own purpose. History is not an accidental sequence or meaningless flow, but a process of the manifestation and fulfillment of His plan. If history were merely an accidental chance, there would be no basis for eternal hope or value in living at all.

Chapter Two

The Divinely Inspired Bible

THE BIBLE IS the most spiritually and practically influential book ever written and is God's final word on salvation. It has been read more widely than any other book in history. Written by thirty-six to forty people from various walks of life, it covers a 1,500-year period from Moses (1440 BC) to the apostle John (AD 90). It consists of thirty-nine books in the Old Testament and twenty-seven books in the New Testament. Irving L. Jensen says the New Testament is God's final revelation of Himself, but that is not to say the Old Testament is obsolete. The New Testament was never intended to replace the Old. Rather, it is the sequel to the Old Testament's origins, heir of its promises, fruit of its seed, the peak of its mountain.[1]

The Holy Spirit inspired all the writers (2 Peter 1:21; 2 Tim. 3:16; Heb. 1:1:1-2). The Bible contains God's universal purpose and character, and His laws, supplying us the answers to questions about the origins of all things, the results of sin, the fall of man, and the plan of salvation in Christ. It defines morality for us and contains narrations from eternity past before creation (John 1:2) to eternity future (Rev. 22:5) with continuity, oneness, and accord.

It leads us to present and future blessing of the eternal kingdom of God in Jesus Christ (Ex. 34:27; Jer. 25:1–25; 3 John 1:2).

Expressions in the Bible such as, "The Lord said," "The word of the Lord came to," and "Jesus said," give full evidence that the whole Bible is the Word of God. There are also many accurate prophecies that did not come by the will of people, who were mostly of illiterate backgrounds, but by the will of God (2 Peter 1:21). Scientists have verified the Word of God by investigation and archaeologists have proven the Word of God by historical discoveries. Incalculable people throughout world history have enjoyed, been impressed by, and have been changed into spiritually new creatures by reading the Word of God. The central theme of the whole Bible is Christ the Savior of sinners (John 1:12). Wayne Grudem says the Bible "refers to the Son of God as 'the Word of God,' and sometimes God's Words take the form of powerful decrees that cause events to happen or even cause things to come into being."[2]

The Bible brings a purposeful hope and a vision of great opportunity. It teaches the spirit of discipline and patience, the value of work and life, and is a firm foundation of eternal faith for our present and future—all through the merits of Jesus Christ (John 14:2–4).

Thomas Carlyle said, "There never was a Book like the Bible and there never will be any other such book."[3] Voltaire, the infidel, said: "Twelve men started Christianity, but one man will destroy it and I will be that one man. Within one hundred years, only a few old Bibles will be found in the museum." Those hundred years have passed, and he was wrong. At an auction sale, the whole of Voltaire's works (ninety-one volumes) were sold for $1.41, while the British government purchased a portion of the Bible, the Codex Sinaiticus, for $700,000, the greatest price ever paid for a book.[4]

The written Bible is "God breathed" and "useful for teaching, rebuking, correcting and training in righteousness" (2 Tim. 3:16) for a practical, holy life on earth as God's children. It is the absolute guide for our present life on earth and eternal future.

The Reliability of the Bible

Truth is based on historical facts. Reliability is based on truth. Therefore, truth brings about reliability. Many have questioned the reliability of the Bible as the Word of God, but there are plenty of evidences to support its reliability. In order to find convincing historical evidence, we depend upon several things: the testimony of eyewitnesses and opposed groups at the time, archaeological evidence, prophetic fulfillments, and finally, the Bible itself.

Eyewitnesses

Eyewitnesses and writers during biblical times came from various backgrounds, locations, and time periods (from about 1440 BC to AD 90), but their themes were consistent throughout the Bible. How could that be, given their varying circumstances, locations and different ages? We see common themes, such as: God as Creator; the fall of man and its effects; the coming Messiah; the birth, life, death, resurrection, and ascension of the Messiah (Christ); His plan of salvation; the second coming of Christ as the Great Judge; and the final judgment.

Some of the eyewitnesses are: Moses (1440 BC); David (1000 BC); Isaiah (740-700 BC); Micah (749-697 BC); Daniel (606-534 BC); Mark (AD 62-68); Matthew (AD 68); Luke (AD 60); John (AD 80-90); Peter (AD 63); James (AD 62); and Paul, the former enemy of Christianity (AD 45-65). There are countless other eyewitnesses. Many Old Testament and New Testament saints were willing to suffer martyrdom for beliefs based on historical fact and their experiences, not just from their own ideas. Many were primary sources and saw the life, torture, and crucifixion of Jesus Christ with their own eyes. Would men be so willing to die for something they believed untrue?

Non-Christian eyewitnesses include, Josephus, a first-century Jewish historian; Cornelius Tacitus, an early second-century Roman historian; Lucian of Samosata, a mid-second century Greek historian; Mara Bar Seyapion, a second- to third-century prisoner; Thallus, and Seneca in the first century. All lived during the time in which Jesus was crucified; many had reasons to muddy the waters but their desire to record their experiences accurately outweighed their own personal biases. We can accept their testimonies about Jesus' crucifixion as accurate.

It is important that so many were eyewitnesses of the crucifixion, resurrection, and ascension of Jesus. Paul recognized that the resurrection is the crux of the Christian faith when he said, "If Christ has not been raised, our preaching is useless and so is your faith" (1 Cor. 15:14). The book of Acts gives us background evidence. Jesus had His doubters. Remember doubting Thomas who said he wouldn't believe unless he saw (John 20:25)? When he touched the resurrected Lord, he fell down and worshipped (John 20:28).

Archaeological Evidence

Archaeology is the study of the material remains of our past. The material remains of the ancient palaces, temples, inscribed stones, coins, and writings allow us to understand the historical, social, cultural, political, economic, and religious backgrounds of the past.

Professor Paul E. Little says more than 25,000 ancient sites showing some connection with the Old Testament period have been located in the Bible lands.[5] Archaeology is an important tool we can use to confirm and verify the reliability of written records, including the Bible. Here are some selected examples.

The Old Testament

The ancient city of Babylon was rebuilt in Iraq. From September 22–October 22, 1987, the Babylon International Festival featuring king Nebuchadnezzar was held at the reconstructed site. The ancient cities of Jerusalem in Israel, Haran in today's southern part of Turkey in Genesis 11:31–32, and Damascus in Syria (Gen. 14:15; Acts 9) currently have the same names. C. L. Wooly discovered Ur, Abraham's hometown (Gen. 11:31), in 1936.[6]

Thousands of tablets discovered by archaeologists at Mari, close to the Euphrates River, give us evidences of similarities to the nomadic culture of the time of Hebrew patriarchs in the Bible. Mark W. Chavalas, a history professor, and K. Lawson Younger, Jr., an Old Testament professor, say, "One area of study that has been explored fairly in recent years is the possible comparisons that could be made between the ancestral narratives of Genesis and the Mari texts that describe the interaction between the government and pastoral nomadic tribal groups."[7] This discovery gives new information about the ancient Mesopotamian cultures and the urban lifestyles of Abraham's time period in relation to the biblical record. The social customs and relationships there paralleled the situations found in the patriarchal society in the Old Testament.

From these excavations we have an idea about patriarchal life, political movements, and cultural and business activities of these cities. More excavated tablets at Nuzi, local east of the city of Mari, show private adoption contracts similar to the situation of Abraham's adoption of Eliezer, and barrenness and remarriage for an heir (Gen. 15–16). According to tablets, the natural son always had the first priority in any situations. A similar case (Gen. 16:1–2) was when Sara, Abraham's wife, who had not borne him children, recommended her husband have a child through her maidservant, Hagar. Alfred Hoerth and John Macray, professors of archaeology, mention a tablet dealing with the right of a married man who has no children. "The man was free to divorce his wife and remarry, but the childless couple also had the option to adopt."[8]

The Old Testament city of Hazor and its king, Jabin, were mentioned in Joshua 11:1, 10. Hazor is about ten miles north of the Sea of Galilee and was one of the largest cities in Israel. It occupied approximately two hundred acres and may have had a population of about thirty thousand people.[9] Hazor, referred to as a center for caravans in the metal trade, and its king's name, Ibni-Addu, are described in excavated Mari tablets. (Abraham Malamat mentions that in the west this would have been pronounced Yabni-Addu, translated from an older Hebrew word, "Yabnu."[10])

We also have records of Jonah's mission to Nineveh. Jonah, the Hebrew prophet, was divinely commissioned to go warn Nineveh to repent. He refused the order and took a trip in the opposite direction. As the book of Jonah (3:5–6) describes, God brought him back to Nineveh and the king of Nineveh repented. "He rose from his throne, took off his royal robes, covered himself with sackcloth and sat down in the dust." Some critics have questioned this event. Did the great Assyrian king get up from his throne, remove his royal robes and sit in the dust? Reports published by the University of Helsinki confirm it to be true. The following quotation is from a letter saying the king must give up fasting: "The king, our Lord, will pardon us. Is one day not enough for the king to mope and to eat nothing? . . . This is the third day [when the king does not eat anything.] The king is beggar."[11]

Then we have the interesting records of the ten plagues in Egypt for Israel's emancipation (Ex. 7–11). Some question whether those plagues actually occurred. Was the water of the Nile River really changed into blood and the firstborn of every Egyptian killed? David K. Down points to "a papyrus written in a later period well kept in the Leiden Museum in Holland which most scholars recognize as being a copy of a papyrus from an earlier dynasty." [12]

The New Testament

The reliability of the New Testament depends primarily upon written documents as evidence. The period covered by New Testament history is too long for archaeology to be as helpful as it is with Old Testament history, which covers a period of about 1,500 years. However, archaeology is still very supportive. For up to twenty years after the ascension of Jesus Christ there were no New Testament books. The first New Testament eyewitness authors were Matthew, Mark, John, Peter, and James. Then came Paul and his companion, Luke. While their original manuscripts were passed from church to church, they were also copied, and then either the originals or copies, or both, would be circulated. Thus, the Gospels and the Epistles could be obtained by individuals and by churches.

The Bible was carefully screened by the early church and church councils for possible mistakes made during copying. Eventually the Bible was canonized. Ever since then it has been relied upon as the inerrant Word of God.

We also have supportive archaeological excavations. When I visited Israel, I found my faith in the Bible was strengthened even more after visiting sites mentioned in the New Testament. Some of them are:

1. Jerusalem with its caves, city walls, and the closed eastern gate wall
2. The Jericho wall (Mark 10:46)
3. The sea of Galilee and the Jordan River
4. The pool of Siloam (John 9:7)
5. The Capernaum synagogue (Matt. 4:13; Mark 1:21, 2:1, 3:1; Luke 4:23)
6. The city of Bethlehem, the birthplace of Jesus Christ
7. The remains of Peter's house
8. The site of Caesarea
9. The tomb of Lazarus in Bethany
10. Gethsemane, the place where Jesus prayed
11. The tomb of Caiaphas
12. The site of the ruins of Laodicea as the last of the seven cities
13. The tomb of Herod.

Fulfilled Prophecies

One of the strongest evidences for the reliability of the Bible is the phenomenon of fulfilled prophecy. The Bible is unique among the religious documentation in that it predicts future events in detail. While the Old Testament can be considered a shadow of the future plans of God, the New Testament is a decisive portion of the realized plans of God through world history in Christ.

According to statistics, out of the Old Testament's 23,210 verses, 6,641 verses are predictive (28.5 percent). In the New Testament, 1, 711 verses out of the total 7,914 verses are predictive (21.5 percent). In the whole Bible (31,124 verses), 8,352 verses are predictive (27 percent).[13]

Fulfilled prophecy proves God is involved in human history. Some prophecies apply to individuals, some to certain locations, some to churches, and some to nations. Some prophecies refer to immediate situations, and some refer to events far in the future. In order to verify the credibility and reliability of the Bible, we have to carefully examine whether the prophecies have been fulfilled or not.

According to Genesis 3, God set the plan of salvation in motion after Adam and Evil fell into sin. The Messiah would come through Abraham's seed. Later, Isaiah says the Messiah will be born of a virgin (Isa. 7:7–14). Isaiah was correct. Here are several more selected biblical prophecies and their realizations as they are related to Christ:

> **Prediction:** One The woman's seed shall bruise the serpent's head, and serpent should bruise his heel. The woman's seed symbolizes Christ, and the serpent's head, Satan. "Heel" refers to Christ's sufferings on the cross.
> **Realization:** The serpent's bruising His heel is a symbolical reference to Christ's suffering and death for our sins. The seed of the woman shall bruise the serpent's head is Christ's resurrection out of the dead and Christ's second coming in person and in power to cast the devil into the bottomless pit (Gen. 3:15, 1440 BC—Rev. 20:2-3, AD 90–96).

> **Prediction:** "Therefore the Lord himself will give you a sign: The virgin will be conceive and give birth to a son, and will call him Immanuel."
> **Realization:** "When the angels had left them and gone into heaven, the shepherds said to one another, "Let's go to Bethlehem and see this thing that has happened, which the Lord has told us about. So they hurried off and found Mary and Joseph, and the baby, who was lying in the manger" (Isa. 7:14, 740-700 BC—Luke 2:15-16, AD 60).

Prediction: "He was oppressed and afflicted, yet he did not open his mouth; he was led like a lamb to the slaughter, and as a sheep before its shearers is silent, so he did not open his mouth."

Realization: "When He was accused by the chief priest and the elders, he gave no answer. Then Pilate asked him, 'Don't you hear the testimony they are bringing against you?' But Jesus made no reply, not even to a single charge—to the great amazement of the governor" (Isa. 53:7, 740–700 BC—Matt. 27:12-14, AD 68).

Prediction: "Rejoice greatly, Daughter Zion! Shout, Daughter Jerusalem! See, your king comes to you, righteous and victorious, lowly and riding on a donkey, on a colt, the foal of a donkey."

Realization: "They brought it to Jesus, threw their cloaks on the colt and put Jesus on it. As he went along, people spread their cloaks on the road. When he came near the place where the road goes down the Mount of Olives, the whole crowd of disciples began joyfully to praise God in loud voices for all the miracles they had seen" (Zech. 9:9, 520–518 BC—Luke 19:35-37, AD 60).

Prediction: "Throw it to the potter"—the handsome price at which they valued me! So I took the thirty pieces of silver and threw them to the potter at the house of the LORD."

Realization: "So Judas threw the money into the temple and left. Then he went away and hanged himself. The chief priests picked up the coins and said . . . 'It is blood money.' So they decided to use the money to buy the potter's field as a burial place for foreigners" (Zech. 11:13, 520–518 BC—Matt. 27:5-7, AD 68).

Prediction: "But he was pierced for our transgressions, he was crushed for our iniquities; the punishment that brought us peace was upon him, and by his wounds we are healed."

Realization: "Then he released Barabbas to them. But he had Jesus flogged, and handed him over to be crucified" (Isa. 53:5, 740–700 BC)—Matt. 27:26 AD 68).

Prediction: "Dogs surround me, a pack of villains encircles me; they pierce my hands and my feet."

Realization: "When they came to the place called the skull, they crucified him, along with the criminals" (Ps. 22:16—Luke 23:33).

Prediction: "They put gall in my food and gave me vinegar for my thirst."

Realization: "There they offered Jesus wine to drink, mixed with gall; but after tasting it, he refused to drink it" (Ps. 69:21, 1440–580 BC—Matt. 27:34, AD 68).

Prediction: "He protects all His bones, not one of them will be broken."

Realization: "These things happened so that the scripture would be fulfilled: 'Not one of his bones will be broken'" (Ps. 34:20, 1440–580 BC—John 19:36, AD 80–92).

The above prophecies about Jesus Christ were fulfilled on earth.

Chapter Three

The Root of Disharmony

WE SEE DISRUPTION of the harmonious order of the world through irregular weather patterns and natural disasters such as hurricanes, earthquakes, etc. (See Gen. 1:2–31.) Earth as our home site is being threatened and damaged today. The world also faces crises created and influenced by mankind of conflicting economic, political, cultural, moral, energy-related, environmental, and religious interests. The root of this imbalance is a higher being which we do not always readily recognize. The Bible reveals the source of the disharmony in this world is a hostile power—the demonic.

The Angelic World

God created angels without physical or material bodies (Luke 24:39). They are special agents that possess high intelligence and power from God. There are fallen angels who used to belong to the good angels. They are not omniscient (2 Pet. 2:11), and they are restricted to exercising their free will within God's appointed boundaries. The Bible speaks of innumerable angels as follows: "But you have come to Mount Zion, to the city of the living God, the heavenly Jerusalem. You have come to thousands upon thousands of angels in joyful assembly" (Heb. 12:22). Unlike mankind, angels were created in a perfect environment of holiness and glory.

The Bible mentions the organization of angels with several special classes, and their boundaries, or orders.

The Names of Angels and Their Ranks

Names: The organization of the "host of heaven" is entrusted to an angel prince (Neh. 9:6; Ps. 148:2, 5). Angels are spirits (Heb. 1:14). Other names for angels are "sons of God" (Job 1:6; 2:1), "holy ones" (Ps. 89:5, 7), "watchers" (Dan. 4:13, 17, 23), "thrones," "dominions," principalities," "authorities" (Col. 1:16), and "powers" (Eph. 1:21). In addition, there are some selected special types of angels.

Types:

The cherubim: The cherubim were given the task of guarding the entrance to the garden of Eden; God frequently traveled with cherubim as His chariot (Ps. 18:10; Ezek. 10:1-22). God appointed cherubim to guard the access to the Tree of Life in the garden of Eden right after Adam's and Eve's fall. God prohibits them from partaking of the Tree of life, and so to live forever, like Satan (Gen. 3:22-24). They were expelled from their earthly paradise under God's eternal plan of salvation.

The Seraphim: They are heavenly beings who are mentioned only in Isaiah 6:2-7 who continually worship the Lord and praise God.

Rank:

Michael: The rank of archangel is held by only one angel (Jude 9). The word *arch* means "chief," so Michael is the prominent leader or commanding officer over all the heavenly angels (Dan. 10:13).

Gabriel: Gabriel is a messenger who comes from God (Dan. 8:16; Luke 1:19), and is the one who bore the message of God concerning the coming kingdom and the King.

Lucifer: Lucifer, "Son of the Morning," has great power and privilege (Isa. 14:12-15). After his fall from heaven, his name became the devil, or Satan (Job 1:6-12, 2:1-7; Matt. 4:10; Rev. 2:24, 3:9, 12:9, 20:2, 7). He is the leader of the fallen angels, the demons.

Lucifer's Fall

The Bible is very clear as to the origin and history of Satan, and his works and destiny. In Isaiah 14:12 there is a reference to the fall of Lucifer (in Latin the word means "light-bearer"), a special prince. He was a beautiful, intelligent creature of God, one of the highest order of angels, an archangel. He possessed great knowledge and power derived from God, but his pride got the best of him and he fell from God's grace (Isa. 14:12-15); Ezek. 28:12-17; Jude 6). After his revolt, he became an adversary of God (1 Peter 5:8), called also the devil or a serpent (Rev. 12:9, 14-15, 20:2). Fallen angels who followed Lucifer are referred to as demons (1 Cor. 10:20-21; 1 Tim. 4:1; James 2:19; Rev. 9:20), or devils and evil spirits with different names (Gen. 3:1-6; Deut. 32:17; Job 1:6; Mark 1:23; 1 Cor. 10:20-21; 2 Cor. 11:3; 1 Tim. 4:1). Lucifer misused his freewill beyond his boundaries in God's service (Isa. 14:12-14; Jude 1:6).

Hostility towards God, and evil influences entered into the universe through Satan and his followers before creation and the fall of Adam and Eve (Gen. 3:1-7, 2:15; Matt. 12:26; Jude 6). Satan and his angels completely lost their privilege of serving God in heaven, and no longer hold their positions as servants of God (Luke 10:18; Jude 6). They were cast out of the heavenly realms into the earth for crossing the prohibited red line of God beyond their positional boundary. The book of Job in the Old Testament and Jude in the New Testament give us a direct clue of this event. (See Rev. 12:12:4; and Isa. 14 for further reference.)

The inhabited earth is called the "cosmos" in the Bible (Rom. 1:8). That is why Satan is called both the "god of this age" (2 Cor. 4:4), "the prince of this world" (John 12:31), and "the prince of the power of the air" (Eph. 2:2), a ruler, and the very first sin-bearer (Dan. 10:13, 20; Eph. 6:12). Even Jesus called Satan the "ruler of the world" (John 12:31, 16:11). The earth is Satan's playground. He is a real person, not an idea or abstract design (1 Peter 5:8). In Genesis 3, Satan, in the form of a serpent, tempted Eve to sin (Gen. 3:1-5). Sometime between the events of Genesis 1:3 and Genesis 3:1, the rebellion in the angelic world with one-third of the angels took place. Lucifer's revolt against God made him the father of lies (John 8:44).

Chapter Four

Understanding Satan's Character and Goal

THROUGHOUT HUMAN HISTORY, evil has had great impact on our lives. Evil instigates disorderly impulses and desires such as lies, hatred, conflict, and immorality. Some ask, "Why does God allow bad things to happen?" The answer to this lies in the free will God has given us.

We need to understand Satan's character and goals as he is the source of evil and its effects. The Bible speaks directly of Satan over two hundred times. Satan's cosmic revolt against God revealed his evil character, his ambitious pride, self-centeredness, and his traits of lying and false accusations (2 Peter 2:11; Jude 9; Ezek. 28:17; John 8:44). His revolt against God caused serious effects, and produced bad consequences. If you punch a concrete wall, your hand will be hurt as a result. We have free choice, but the results will remain forever with us. The violation of God's law is sin. L. S. Chafer defines evil and sin as follows: "Evil refers to what, though latent and not expressed, is conceivable as the opposite of what is good. Sin is what is concrete and actively opposed to the character of God."[1]

When Christ returns, all questions about evil will disappear and we will understand clearly (1 Cor. 13:12). Satan has exercised his power to damage the world since the fall of Adam and Eve. Because his world is above and around the earth, he tries to oppose God's authority and to destroy His spiritual system and its rule (Eph. 2:2, 6:12). His evil weapons of deception, temptation, pride, and a denial of the power of God are rampant in our world. We cannot account for people's actions without recognizing the influence of evil behind the actions. Satan will continue to work through people to destroy God's harmonious system until his last eternal punishment by God (Rev. 20:10).

However, Satan cannot upset the fundamental stability of the universe created by God. God will prevail. Satan and his followers will not descend to hell until Christ casts them into the lake of fire after their final rebellion at the end of the millennium (Rev. 20:1–15). Even now, Satan's power is growing in the world. The following are Satan's main goals:[2]

- To deny the existence of God the Creator in the name of scientific knowledge
- Get people to believe they are autonomous and unaccountable to God
- Convince people that moral absolutes do not exist.
- Let people believe that all religions are the pathway to heaven.
- Distract people so they place a higher priority on themselves, rather than the kingdom of God
- Tempt people to focus on the now, rather than eternal life.

The Bible warns us to be alert and sober minded as the devil is looking for those he can devour (1 Peter 5:8–9).

Chapter Five

The Completion of Creation

HUMANS ARE GOD'S most valuable masterpieces. God placed Adam and Eve in the paradise land of Eden, which means "pleasure land and loveliness." They were made in the unique image and likeness of God (Gen. 1:26–27). "The fact that man is in the image of God means that man is like God and represents God."[1] This does not mean identical to God, but similar in ways of limited intellectual and creative abilities, moral decisions, and free will.

James Wire says that like God, we have personality, self-transcendence, intelligence (the capacity for reason and knowledge), morality (the capacity for recognizing and understanding good and evil), social capacity (our characteristic and fundamental desire and need for human companionship), and creativity (the ability to imagine new things or endow old things with human significance).[2]

Theologian Wayne Grudem says human beings "in many ways represent God."[3] Because we reflect the Creator in many ways, we are God's earthly mission agents. God commanded

Adam, "Be fruitful, and multiply, and replenish the earth, and subdue it" (Gen. 1:28 KJV).

Ancient Greek philosophers believed man was primarily a spirit and a body and that the body is a lower order of reality. Materialists without God believe man is simply a product of nature; therefore, a person is treated only as a part of the material substance of society, not as an important and valuable individual. As Adam's descendants, our dignity and value is from God. We are divine vessels for divine grace and for conforming to God's image. We are equipped with the faculties of free will, intelligence, morality, and emotion.

We are also task-oriented beings. God created us with a spirit, a soul, and a body (1 Thess. 5:23). In contrast to the material part of us, God breathed into man the immaterial part of human beings. God imparted something of His own nature into us (Gen. 1:27). God distinguishes the spirit of a person from his soul (Gen. 2:7) and He placed this soul in a created earthen body. In general, the soul seems to relate primarily to psychological or natural experiences and reveals our personalities. The spirit, by contrast, seems to relate more to religious experience. The physical body comes into contact with the material world.

Our intellect, as a part of the soul, helps us understand mysteries of all kinds, and our emotions are for enjoying abundant life. In addition, the soul reveals our personality. If our human spirit complies with God's Word, then our soul rules over our passions, and we can rule over the world as earthly representatives of God. In this sense we are God's masterpiece. However, in order for us to carry out our mission, we must remain faithful to God.

Satan's Attack on Man

God gave man dominion over the earth with one rule: do not eat of the Tree of the Knowledge of Good and Evil. Adam was "to till and to keep or guard" the garden. This shows us there must have been a dangerous force present that made such a "guarding" necessary. God told Adam the consequences of disobedience would be death (Gen. 2:17).

God designed a world where all peoples are destined to live under His law. Galatians 6:7 says, "A man reaps what he sows." If a man sows laziness in his work, he will reap poverty.

Satan appeared to Eve in the form of a serpent to tempt her with a cunning, deceptive question (Gen. 3; Rev. 12:9). The serpent twisted God's command, and appealed to Eve's natural desire for wisdom to make herself like God. Eve accepted Satan's deceptive idea by eating the forbidden fruit, and she brought it to her husband Adam and he ate it. Even though Satan did not directly deceive Adam, both sinned and became transgressors. That one sin was passed on to all of humanity, and Satan has been tempting mankind ever since.

Satan cannot be seen with our physical eyes, but we can see his evil activities working through mankind. He is irretrievably an evil, malevolent creature. Satan's attempts continue to turn people away from God by prompting the importance of our egos, tempting us to participate in idol worship (Lev. 17:7; Deut. 32:17; Ps. 106:36–38); false teachings; and by causing people to worship Satan himself (Rev. 13:1–18). His goal is to destroy the integrity and glorious authority of God's command, and what God creates and loves. He is against God because he lost his position in heaven. Consequently, when anyone becomes a faithful believer, Satan begins a constant warfare with him or her.

Consequences of Adam and Eve's Sin

The results of disobeying God's command brought sin and death into the human race. The line of Adam and Eve's relationship with God was totally broken. Their decision-making processes and morality was warped and damaged. The presence of evil and sinful practices within humanity stem from Adam and Eve's acceptance of Satan's deceptive idea for their selfish interests and glory.

Sin is a side-effect of Adam and Eve's violation of God's rules (cause). In Adam, a sinful nature has been passed on to us. Accordingly, sin is manifested in the nature of all humans (effects). Theologian Millard J. Erickson explains the roots of sin from Adam and Eve by saying, "Consequently, all of us begin life with a natural tendency to sin, and the Bible tells us that with the fall, man's first sin, a radical change took place in the universe."[4] As a result, mankind still experiences as side-effects spiritual alienation from God, ruin of the soul, physical death, evil thoughts, rejection of God, idolatry, impurity, theft, murder, lying, false witnesses, greed, malice, deceit, slanders, adultery, fornication, arrogance, hatred, brutality, factions, physical pleasure-seekers, abusiveness, and the like (Mark 7:20–22; Gal. 5:19-20; James 3:14; 2 Tim. 3:1–5).

People continue to be affected positively and negatively by their use of free will. Adam and Eve's sin was the beginning of all the tragedies that Satan helped instigate. Some of the effects of disobeying God's commands are:

God's image, their spiritual DNA, was extremely distorted.
They lost the spiritual privilege of walking closely with God.
They lost their paradise of Eden.
They would encounter physical and spiritual death.
Their sins passed on to the whole human race.
Women endure pain during labor.
The ground is cursed because of Adam's sin.
Men must do painful toil to eat.

Chapter Six

God's Redemptive
Work on Earth

The Selection of a Common Man

GOD'S ETERNAL PURPOSES and faithfulness to His chosen people did not change after the fall of Adam and Eve. God's grace and blessings, judgments and redemption continue to this day. God unconditionally called Abraham, a man living in today's southern Iraq, to leave his hometown in quest of a new land. God began a completely new age through Abraham and his descendants by setting them apart from the spiritually and morally polluted world to be a channel of His salvation to the nations.

Abraham accepted God's call without question (Gen. 12:1-4); as a result, Abraham and his family were blessed. Abraham's grandson's name was changed from Jacob to Israel, so his sons became the children of Israel, and their descendants Israelites. In Jacob's twelve sons a broad foundation was laid for the future development of the nation. They were separated, protected, and preserved with the gift of the Promised Land.

But Israel did not adhere to God's laws. This started when God's people were held captive in Egypt for a period of 430 years.

When they were freed and traveling to the Promised Land, they turned to idolatry (Ezek. 16 and 23). Later they faced seventy years in captivity in Babylonia, just as Jeremiah prophesied (Jer. 25:11-12, 29:10). Some of the people were released from their captivity under King Cyrus (2 Chron. 36:22-23) who defeated the Babylonians in 536 BC. They were carrying on the rites of temple worship but had fallen into a spiritually backslidden condition.

They did not honor God (Mal. 1:6), but continued to hold out for the promised Messiah (Isa. 7:14). They fell again into a period of spiritual darkness, the so-called 400 silent years without any messages from God through His chosen prophets, after the prophet Malachi (445-397 BC). God's faithfulness to His chosen people shows how closely He is involved in human history. Abraham's descendants could have reaped great blessings, but they failed to answer God's call and adhere to His expectations.

The descendants of Abraham lost their freedom and became subjected to the Roman Empire (AD 70); they were dispersed among the nations for over 1,800 years, as the prophets prophesied (Lev. 26:21-39; Deut. 28:12-25, 64). Jerusalem, the holy city, was trodden down by the nations as God's judgment (Matt. 23:35-38, 27:25) until its rebirth on May 14, 1948.

God's promises have been fulfilled through history. The prophecies of the Old Testament promised a coming Messiah (1 Chron. 17:13; Ps. 110:1). Then God sent His Son, Jesus Christ into this world in human flesh for human salvation through the promised virgin birth as Isaiah predicted (Gen. 3:15; Isa. 7:14; 9:6 (740-700 BC). This took place at the appointed place of Micah's prediction (Micah 5:2, 749-697 BC). This is the sign of God's direct involvement in human history.

Chapter Seven

The Beginning of End Times

THIS IS THE end-time stage of human history. The last days began with the first appearance of Jesus Christ into this world. (See Acts 2:16–17; 1 Tim. 3:1; Heb. 9:26; 1 Pet. 1:20; 1 John 2:18.) The last days will end with His second coming to this world. The period between Christ's first and His second appearance is called the day of salvation, or the day of grace, or the church age (2 Cor. 6:2).

Christ's direct words about the last days are found in John 6:39, 40, 44, 54; 12:48).

Who is Jesus Christ?

Jesus Christ is the Son of God who came into this world. Religious leaders theoretically knew the prediction of the Messiah's coming by virgin birth, but did not believe it because of their spiritual blindness. Many people today have a hard time believing Christ was born of a virgin. Christ came into human history in a miraculous way to restore and save all who accept Him as Lord. Jesus Christ, came to this world as both man and

God through the virgin birth. God is the almighty Creator, so in Him, everything is possible.

Jesus Christ stepped into a corrupt society and preached repentance of sin, and the nearness of God's kingdom (Isa. 49:6; Matt. 4; John 3:16-17). Christ showed us who He is by healing many people, and casting demons out with amazing authority. Jesus associated with a hated tax collector, sinners, the poor, the crippled, the blind, and Gentiles. He healed a person with leprosy and talked with a Samaritan woman who was rejected by her neighbors because of her serial marriages. Jesus' mission went beyond the Jewish boundaries (Matt. 9:12-13). He said no one could enter the kingdom except through him.

Jesus told the Jews to repent, emphasizing inner purity over external purity. The fate of all people is dependent upon their acceptance or rejection of Him as Savior, not on tradition. Here is who Christ is:

> He existed before Abraham (John 8:58).
> He is equal with the Father in heaven (John 5:17-18; 10:25-33).
> He has the authority to forgive sins (Mark 2:5-7).
> He is God (John 10:33, 16:15, 15:23, 8:12).
> He has authority to give eternal life (John 17:2).
> He is the resurrection and the life (John 11:25).
> He came to this world to give His life as a ransom for many (Matt. 20:28).
> He is the way, the truth, and the life (John 14:6).

Jewish religious leaders questioned Christ's true identity, teachings and claims. They followed Him and kept asking about His true identity to try to entrap Him. Judas, one of Christ's disciples, betrayed Him for profit and handed Him over to the head of the Jewish authority. When they asked Christ about His identity he said, "I am the One who is sent by the Father, and I am the Son of God." He was accused of blasphemy, and false accusations were made, but no base for a charge against Him was found.

Christ was sentenced to be crucified (Matt. 27; Luke 23). Roman soldiers took Christ's clothes off and put a purple robe on Him. While some pressed a crown of thorns hard down upon His head, others mocked Him by calling Him, "Hail, King of the Jews!" He was scourged and spit upon, and totally betrayed by His chosen people. Even while Christ's hands and feet were nailed to a wooden cross, the chief priests, teachers of the law, and the elders mocked Him. When a Roman soldier pierced His side with a spear, out flowed blood and water.

Behind the Jewish authorities and the Roman soldiers, there was the involvement of Satan who craftily manipulated people's sinful nature to do evil.

The Significance of Christ's Death

Christ's death on the cross as the sinless Son of God is the greatest event in human history (see John 3:16–18). Christ stepped into this world to save mankind from his sins so we could avoid eternal judgment. Sinful man cannot save sinful man. Only the sinless God-man, Jesus Christ, could save sinful man from his sins (Rom. 3:25–26). If Jesus had not been a man, He could not have died in man's place and paid the penalty for the sin of all mankind. Charles Ryrie says, "God stepped into a hopeless situation and provided a vicar in Jesus Christ who did provide an eternal satisfaction for sin."[1]

His death on the cross was a substitute sacrifice for sinners so we might enter the kingdom of heaven (Matt. 20:28). His death on the cross is the great expression of the love and grace of God the Father (John 3:16; Heb. 2:10; Rom. 5:8), and also satisfies the justice of God (Rom. 3:25–27). Rejection of Christ is rejection the grace and love of God the Father. Those who do not accept Him as their Savior are eternally lost. There can be no salvation without Christ's sacrifice.

Jesus Christ opened a universal way of forgiveness as a priceless treasure of His love and grace so those who are undeserving can come to Him by faith. Christ's earthly redemptive mission has been completed; the full price has been paid. Christ Jesus took judgment in His own physical body to open a way of forgiveness for those who accept Christ as their personal Savior. Through God's endless grace, all we have to do to have eternal life is to accept Him as our personal Savior (Matt. 20:28). Philip Yancey says, "Grace means there is nothing we can do to make God love us more and there is nothing we can do to make God love us less."[2]

Big Questions

Why did the Son of God accept the death penalty on the cross? Why did He not use His divine supernatural power to punish those who made false accusations and condemned Him to death?

First, we must realize God the Father did not need to save any people at all. Our heavenly Father is love (John 3:16) and justice (Rom. 3:25–26). He is loving, gracious, and merciful. He doesn't rejoice in the judgment and punishment of man's sin, but He is also just. His justice comes from His holiness, and righteousness. So, His justice cannot get along with sin, and does not allow forgiveness of man's sin without a penalty being paid. His ultimate grace and His love moved Him to save sinful man. Christ fully obeyed God's will by satisfying His justice (Matt. 20:28). Without God's justice, Jesus Christ could not offer the privilege of salvation to man. Rejection of Christ's death on the cross is rejection of God's endless grace and love, which causes God's righteous judgment.

Chapter Eight

Defeating the Power of Death

THE UNPRECEDENTED RESURRECTION of Jesus Christ has been a sensitive issue throughout the ages. The Bible speaks of this as a factual event. The disciples of Christ, His followers, and the converted apostle Paul were eyewitnesses of this event, and are reliable sources. Let's examine the issue of the credibility of the resurrection of Jesus Christ.

The Testimonies of Transformed Eyewitnesses

The primary important evidence for Jesus' resurrection is the biblical narrative. Uniquely, the testimonies of Mary Magdalene, and other women who first arrived at the empty burial tomb of Jesus Christ, give us factual and convincing evidence. The empty tomb means Jesus Christ rose from the dead. He showed himself to Peter, the other disciples, to Thomas, to James, and to five hundred brethren at once (1 Cor. 15:6), to a group of disciples, and to His followers. Mary, the mother of Jesus, and the other women had indeed seen Christ's crucifixion and burial, and all of them witnessed the ascension from the Mount of Olives near Jerusalem.

Later, on the road to Damascus to arrest Christians, Saul (Paul) experienced the risen Christ. Christ's resurrection transformed His disciples. After Jesus' ascension into heaven, Peter boldly preached the message of the risen Christ (Acts 1:12, 2:1-47). He told government authorities, "We cannot help speaking what we have seen and heard" (Acts 4:20). Peter's change from his past behavior proves that Christ's resurrection is true.

Peter: Before the resurrection of Jesus Christ, Peter denied Jesus three times. After the resurrection, Peter encountered the risen Christ and talked to him (John 21:15-17). Peter personally bore witness that Jesus rose from the dead (Acts 2:32).

John: John testified that he had seen with his eyes, and had touched Christ who had appeared to him and others (1 John 1:1-2).

James: Jesus' brother was a strong skeptic. As one of Jesus' half brothers, he did not believe in Jesus as the Savior during the years of His public ministry (Acts 1:14; John 7:2-8). Christ's resurrection definitely changed him and he became the main leader of the Christians, next to Peter (Acts 15:12-21; Gal. 1:19; 1 Cor. 9:5). James was martyred for Christ, according to Josephus, the Jewish historian (AD 64-93).[1]

Thomas: One of the twelve disciples, he doubted the resurrection. When Jesus physically appeared to a group of the disciples, he had opportunity to see the nail marks and touch His side. Christ affirmed the reality of His resurrection to Thomas (John 20:25-29).

Stephen: He was stoned for believing Jesus (Acts 6; 7:59-60).

Paul: He was a fanatical, anti-Christian religious leader who persecuted the church after Christ's ascension. He experienced the risen Christ on the road to Damascus (1 Cor. 15:8; Acts

9:3–22). He became a key servant of God, wrote much of the New Testament, and was martyred for his faith by Nero, the emperor of Rome around AD 66.

The disciples: They were direct eyewitnesses of Christ's resurrection who were totally changed afterwards and willingly faced cruel persecution and death for preaching the gospel (Acts 1:9). All were martyred except the apostle John. "Peter was crucified upside down; James, the half brother of Jesus, was stoned; Matthew was killed by the sword; James, son of Alphaeus, was crucified; James, son of Zebedee, was killed by the sword; Thaddaeus was killed by being shot with arrows; Bartholomew was crucified; Andrew was crucified; Philip was crucified; Simon the Zealot was crucified; Thomas was killed with spear; Paul was beheaded."[2]

Why would they face cruel persecution and death if Christ was not the true Son of God? Who would willingly die for something that was not true? They surely believed that Jesus Christ was the Son of God who proved who this through His resurrection.

Testimonies of the Early Church Leaders

We have a wide range of sources for the historical life of Christ found in the writings of those who followed on the heels of the very first apostles. Some were church leaders, teachers, and apologists, who believed Jesus was the Son of God as revealed in the Bible. Here is a selection of leaders who wrote of the historical life of Jesus Christ from AD 100 and 200.

Clement of Rome was a disciple of Peter and Paul and the head of the Roman congregation at the close of the first century. He was appointed by Peter to be bishop of Rome, as his successor. He died as a martyr at sea.[3] Clement wrote of being "fully assured through the resurrection of our Lord Jesus Christ."[4]

Symeon was bishop of Jerusalem, and like his predecessor James, a kinsman of Jesus, was accused by fanatical Jews, and crucified in AD 107 at the age of a hundred and twenty years.[5]

Ignatius (AD 50–115) was the head of the church of Antioch, the mother church of Gentile Christianity at the close of the first century. He was "thrown to lions in the Coliseum for the amusement of the people because of his faith in Jesus Christ."[6] Ignatius wrote seven epistles on the way from Antioch to Rome.[7] In one of his letters on the way to Rome he wrote of Christ as "Son of God by the Divine will and power" and mentioned the resurrection.[8]

Quadratus was a disciple of the apostles, and bishop of Athens, and an early apologist. Eusebius, a church historian, quoted Quadratus' writing on the miracles of Christ, those who were healed and those raised from the dead.[9]

Aristides was an eloquent philosopher at Athens who is mentioned by Eusebius as a contemporary of Quadratus. A fragment of his defense of Christianity, addressed to Roman emperor Hadrian, shows the preaching of Paul had taken root in Athens. He described Jesus Christ as: "the Son of the most high God, revealed by the Holy spirit, descended from heaven, born of a Hebrew Virgin. His flesh He received from the Virgin, and He revealed Himself in the human nature as the Son of God . . . He was crucified, being pierced with nails by the Jews; and He rose from the dead and ascended to heaven."[10]

Polycarp of Smyrna, a disciple of the apostle John, presided as presbyter-bishop over the church of Smyrna in Asia Minor in the first half of the second century. Polycarp steadfastly refused to deny his Savior and in the flames praised God for having deemed him worthy "to be numbered among his martyrs."[11]

Justin, the philosopher and martyr, became an earnest Christian in his youth, and an outstanding writer in defense of Christianity. Refusing to worship idols, he was whipped and then beheaded in Rome about 165.[12]

The New Day of Christian Worship

Another convincing evidence for the resurrection of Jesus Christ is the change of the day of regular Christian worship from the Jewish Sabbath (Saturday) to Sunday, the first day of the week. The Jewish religious tradition for worship has always been being practiced on the last day of the week, the day of God's rest after His finishing His creation. The new Christians suddenly and uniformly began to worship on Sunday though it was an ordinary workday (Acts 20:7). The only adequate cause is they wanted to commemorate the resurrection of Jesus Christ on the first day of the week.

Non-Christians' Records about the Crucifixion and Resurrection of Jesus Christ

We can find the descriptions of the crucifixion of Jesus Christ in the four Gospels, but also in non-Christian sources.

Josephus, as the leading Jewish historian (AD 64–94) said, "Now there was about this time, Jesus, a wise man, if it be lawful to call him a man, for he was a doer of wonderful works . . . He drew over to him both many of the Jews, and many of the Gentiles. He was Christ; and when Pilate, at the suggestion of the principle men among us, had condemned Him to the cross, those that loved Him at the first did not forsake Him, for He appeared to them alive again the third day, as divine prophets had foretold these."[13]

Seneca, a Roman philosopher and politician in the first century, described Jesus' crucifixion as a man hanging on the cross appearing "sickly," "deformed," and swollen with "ugly welts on the shoulders and chest."[14]

Cornelius Tacitus (AD 64–116) was a reliable Roman historian who wrote, "The persons commonly called Christians, who were hated for their enormities. Christus, the founder of the name, was put to death by Pontius Pilate, procurator of Judea in the reign of Tiberius: but the pernicious superstition, repressed for a time broke out again, not only through Judea, where the mischief originated, but through the city of Rome also."[15]

Hadrian, the emperor of Rome from AD 117 to 138, wrote concerning the punishment of Christians.[16]

Thallus, the Samaritan-born historian, mentions Christ in his book of histories as "a matter of fact."[17]

Pontius Pilate was deeply involved in Christ's crucifixion. We read about him in the four Gospels of the Bible. He is also in the historical record: "He was 5th Roman procurator in Judea after the deposition of Archelaus in AD 6."[18]

The Place of the Cross

Christ's death on the cross is the centerpiece of the gospel. The Bible's description of the location is historically and geographically true. The name of the place is Golgotha which means "a skull," and "calvary" in Latin. It was a hill unprotected by the city walls of Jerusalem and a place of death just outside the city of Jerusalem. Hebrews 13:12–13 describes this location: "And so Jesus also suffered outside the city gate to make the people holy through His own blood. Let us, then, go to him outside the camp, bearing the disgrace he bore."

The Impact of Christ's Resurrection on Christian Faith

Christ's resurrection gives us a joyous and captivating eternal hope. Even though death is an inescapable reality of life on earth, it is not the end for believers and unbelievers. After death there is eternal life—either in heaven or in hell. Christ was the first to have an eternally resurrected body. So, all believers who died in Christ will be resurrected when He comes again to judge the world (1 Thess. 4:14–17; 2 Peter 3:7; Rev. 14:7).

Christ conquered the power of death. Our faith rests on His resurrection. It tells us death is not the end of man's existence, but a stepping-stone for believers. Jesus Christ is the eternal God, the living light for mankind. Christ's substitutional death on the cross and His resurrection is the cornerstone of salvation. His resurrection gives us the foundation of our faith, hope, and the proof of God's love for us.

Here's what the resurrection means to us.

- The resurrection of Jesus Christ proves Jesus Christ is the Son of God by validating His claims to be the Lord and Messiah (Acts 2:36).
- The resurrection of Jesus Christ proves God exists outside of time and is not bound by it.
- Death was conquered only by Jesus Christ.
- Christ bodily coming back from the dead is totally outside the range of natural laws.
- The resurrection proves the God of the Bible is the true God of creation.
- The resurrection shows God's endless love to save His created people from sin.
- The resurrection proves Jesus Christ is the only Savior of the world.
- Christianity is based on the bodily resurrection of Jesus Christ (John 8:58, 10:30).
- The resurrection of Jesus Christ completes salvation for those who believe in Him as Savior.
- The resurrection of Jesus Christ profoundly and continually impacts civilization.
- The resurrection of Jesus Christ proves He is the Creator and the source of life (John 1:1–3, 14:6).

Chapter Nine

The Consequences of Rejection of Jesus Christ

The Birth of the Church as a New Spiritual Community

AFTER CHRIST'S ASCENSION into heaven, His disciples and followers in Jerusalem received the power of the Holy Spirit at Pentecost (John 20:22; Acts 2:1–4). This spiritual experience was an amazing event in history. Their hearts then burned for evangelizing the world according to Christ' command (Matt. 28:18–20). The church as Christ's spiritual body began reaching out to others with the gospel.

The early Christians gladly received the apostles' teaching and met in heartfelt fellowship, the breaking of bread, and deep prayer. Everyone was filled with awe, and the apostles did many wonders and miraculous signs. All the believers had everything in common. Selling their possessions and goods, they gave to anyone as he had need. Every day they continued to meet together in the temple courts. With glad and sincere hearts, they praised God and enjoyed the favor of all the people. New believers were daily added.

Their message focused on Christ's identity, death on the cross for the sin of mankind, His resurrection, ascension into heaven, and how acceptance of Him as Savior was needed for eternal life. This message, preached by the apostles Peter, John, and Paul, and many others, advanced through Jerusalem and neighbor nations, and went from land to land. Peter began in Jerusalem (Acts 2–12); John went out to Ephesus and western Asia Minor (Rev. 2:3); Paul moved from Antioch out among nations (Acts 13–28).

God is going to fulfill His redemptive plans through the church. Wayne Grudem says, "The community of all the believers for all time, and the picture of the church as God's temple should increase our awareness of God's presence dwelling in our midst as we meet and begin to experience the blessing of God's rule in their lives."[1]

The church is a heavenly light shining in the darkness of the world (Phil. 2:15) and a spiritual community of Christ on a hill that cannot be hidden (Matt. 5:14–16). The church, instead of Israel, is commissioned to give the salvation message to the world. As the proclaimer and interpreter of Christ's message, the church has been steadily advancing the kingdom of God through the ages. God has entrusted His church with the gospel and has promised not even the gates of hell will succeed in stopping it.

The World Mission Task

What are the consequences of Israel's national rejection of Jesus Christ? Jesus Christ was rejected by the people of Israel as the result of an organized plot of the religious leaders. Their rejection brought the serious consequences of the loss of their country. The temple was destroyed and numerous inhabitants in Jerusalem were killed by the Romans under the leadership of Titus around AD 70. The legions of Rome killed over one and a quarter million of its inhabitants.[2] This dispersed the people who met persecution everywhere they went.

The fifteenth and sixteenth centuries were tragic periods for the scattered people of Israel, especially during the Inquisition.[3] The pogroms in Russia brought tremendous persecution against Jewish people. This persecution continued in Germany in World War II, where six million Jews were massacred under the Hitler regime. Hitler had women's hair cut off and used in the manufacturing of clothing and mattresses. The few who survived these horrors have told stories of unspeakable things.

Why was this allowed to happen? Matthew 23:37–38 says:

> Jerusalem, Jerusalem, you who kill the prophets and stone those sent to you, how often I have longed to gather your children together, as a hen gathers her chicks under her wings, and you were not willing, look your house is left to you desolate.

The religious leaders of Israel said, "His blood is on us and on our children!" (Matt. 27:25). Israel was commissioned to carry God's salvation plan to the world as God's agent on earth, but they continually fell short. The Bible predicted the hardships and dispersions of Israel for refusing to listen to God and rejecting Him.

In Leviticus 26:21–39 it says the "afflictions" would be multiplied seven times over, wild animals would attack, they would be scattered among the nations, and the land "laid waste," and cities in ruin. In Deuteronomy 28:12–25, 64, the punishment for disobedience included curses overtaking them (Deut. 28:12–25, 64), being scattering among the nations (Jer. 9:13–16), pursued with the sword, and famine and plague coming upon them (Jer. 29:18–19). They would be driven among the nations where they would be "an object of cursing and horror, of scorn and reproach." Hosea 9:17 says, "My God will reject them because they have not obeyed him; they will be wanderers among the nations."

Matthew 24:2 predicted the temple would be destroyed. They would be "taken as prisoners to all the nations. Jerusalem will be trampled on by the Gentiles until the times of the Gentiles are fulfilled" (Luke 21:20-24). Until this day, part of Jerusalem belongs to Palestine.

God has always been involved in human history and He speaks in advance to the world before His actions. Israel is God's firstborn among the family of nations and had greater responsibilities. Their scattering was literal, but they were permitted to remain some forty years after Christ's crucifixion. We, also, must not ignore God's warnings.

In spite of the rejection of Christ by Israel, God's promised purpose for Israel has not changed (Rom. 11:1). God had an eternal plan for them to return to their homeland. On May 14, 1948, Israel initiated their declaration of independence. For the first time in two thousand years the Jews had a home again. This was an unimaginable miracle! God's promise to bring back Israel to their homeland was spoken through Moses (Deut. 30:2-5), Jeremiah (30:10), Ezekiel (11:11-17, 34:12, 36:24, 37:12), Amos (9:14-15), and Zephaniah (3:20).

Salvation has come to the Gentiles (Rom. 11:25) to provoke Israel to jealousy (Acts 9:15; Rom. 11:11-15). God's plan for the present or church age is not the transforming of the human race and the establishing of Christian nations. God wants His chosen people to accept Christ as their Savior through the church (John 6:37, 39, 44; 11: 27; 13:18; Acts 15:14). We are living in the "last day" of the last days, the grace period for the believers.

How Long Will Israel's Rejection by God Last?

Israel was commissioned to carry God's redemptive plan to the world, but they have continually fallen short. The restoration of the kingdom (national Israel) is only a question of "times or dates." In Romans 11:1 the apostle Paul said God's faithful promised purpose for Israel and through Israel has not changed.

When the Jews returned again to their Promised Land on May 14, 1948, they were still in unbelief of Christ as their Messiah. At present the number of Jews accepting Christ is growing. In Jeremiah 30:10 the Lord declares He will save their "descendants from the land of their exile." Ezekiel 11:17 says Israel will be gathered from the nations. Again in Ezekiel 36:24 and 37:12 it is promised they would be brought back to Israel. Amos 9:14–15 says they would be planted in their own land, "never again to be uprooted." Their captivity would be turned back, and they would be "a name and a praise among all the people of the earth" (Zeph. 3:20).

God has been involved in Israel's history every step of the way. So we can conclude the Christian faith is not based on blind and theoretical faith, but on the true facts of God's involvement. Our eternal salvation comes through Jesus Christ who came back to life from the dead.

Jesus Christ is the Son of God who came into human history to save us. If the apostles Peter and Paul were real people in history, then Christ is true. Israel's loss of their land was rooted in the rejection of Jesus Christ. The rebirth of national Israel by God's direct involvement proves the God of the Bible is truly alive and active.

Chapter Ten

The Expectation of Christ's Return

Signs of the Last Days

THE PRESENT PERIOD is outlined in the New Testament as the "last days" and the "church age." The last days began with Christ's first coming into the world (Heb. 1:2, 9:26; 1 Peter 1:20) and covers the entire period from the first to the second coming of Christ. Jesus and His disciples used the expressions "last day" (John 6:39, 40, 44, 54; 12:48). The "last days" have already lasted around two thousand years. The Bible gives us predictions as to how world events will move toward their final end. The last days are characterized by the outpouring of the Holy Spirit at Pentecost, a fulfillment of Joel's prophecy (Acts 2:16–17). Before Christ's ascension, He clearly prophesied the coming of the Holy Spirit and believers being witnesses to the whole world (Acts 1:8). We now are approaching the "last" of the last days.

Big Signs of the Last Days

The Bible is a spiritual road map that provides road conditions for our safety and security. Here are some of the biblical warning signs for the last days:

Matthew 24:3-11 warns of nation rising against nation, famines, earthquakes, persecution, hatred of Christians, backsliding, and false prophets. Matthew 24:12 tells of the love of many growing cold because of the increase of wickedness. Acts 2:17-20 promises God will pour out His Spirit, with attending visions and dreams, and prophecy. There will be wonders such as blood, fire, the sun being turned to darkness, and the moon to blood. John 14:2-3 says Jesus is preparing a place for us to be with Him. In 2 Corinthians 4:3-4 the blindness of the minds of unbelievers is foretold.

God's plan for the present age is to invite sinners to become part of the body of Christ (John 6:37, 39, 44; 11:27; 13:18; Acts 15:14). Some of the chosen people of Israel will come to Jesus Christ and become part of the church (Rom. 11:1-7). The ruler of the kingdom of the air (the devil) is now at work in those who are disobedient (Eph. 2:2). The consummation of history will end up with God's judgment: "That day will bring about the destruction of the heavens by fire, and the elements will melt in the heat" (2 Peter 3: 12b).

The Literal Restoration of Israel

Israel's national restoration was spoken by the Old Testament, and by implication by Jesus Christ and the apostle Paul (Deut. 30:2-5; Jeremiah 30:10; Ezekiel 11:17, 34:12, 36:24, 37:12; Amos 9:14-15; Zeph. 3:20; Acts 1:6; Romans 11:1-5). Amos 9:14-15 says Israel will never again be uprooted; Romans 11:1-5 says God did not reject His people and speaks of a "remnant chosen by grace."

From the history of Israel on earth, we learn that God is the "controller" of history. God's purpose for Israel has not changed; their scattering was not permanent. It was literal, and the return to the Promised Land was also literal, exactly as the prophecies foretold. God blesses Gentile Christians through Israel. God's salvation message came to Israel through Jesus, indirectly blessing the Gentiles through Israel. The direct affliction of God on the Gentiles came from Him, and the indirect affliction on Israel came through the Gentiles. Just as the God of the Bible has chastised Israel through the instrument of the Gentiles, so God will do much more to Gentiles if they do not accept Jesus Christ as their Savior. The time of salvation for the Gentiles seems to be running out (Rom. 11:25).

The Increase of Human Knowledge

The Bible prophesied an increase of man's knowledge in the end times. Daniel, a Jewish prophet who lived approximately 618–534 BC, received a revelation of the end time from God (Dan. 2:48, 5:29, 6:3, 28). Today is the age of increasing knowledge and information just as Daniel prophesied. Our daily lives are being reshaped by the development and increase of technological knowledge and information. The Internet allows us to connect to various knowledge and information sources and to communicate with what others, turning Planet Earth into a global village.

This high-tech culture is producing new thinking patterns, but also is taking away the ability of deep thinking; interactions with others are becoming increasingly impersonal. Many treat this advanced scientific knowledge as an idol, and embrace a materialistic worldview.

Chapter Eleven

The Unmasked Power on the Scene

THEORIES VARY ON the origin of all things. Those who believe in creation believe God is the first cause. The Bible starts with this declaration, "In the beginning God created the heavens and the earth" (Gen. 1:1). Creationists believe the Creator is the ultimate source of everything; that the world consists of complex systems with interrelatedness and interdependence toward a certain goal; that all creatures reproduce only after their own kind—monkeys come from monkeys; watermelons from watermelon seeds.

Those who hold to the theory of evolution believe that both organic and inorganic things appear in order of increasing complexity. So the creationist position and the evolutionary position are totally different from their starting points. The creationist view has an inspired written record, the Bible, and many careful investigations support the trustworthiness of this view. The evolutionary notion of origin doesn't have the slightest bit of empirical evidence.

The Evolutionary View

According to the theory of evolution, the beginning of life was an accidental event that arose from a self-existent non-living material. Through natural selection, uniquely combined chemicals evolved over massive amounts of time into increasingly complex organisms, selecting variants among species from lower to higher forms of life. Presumably, mutations occurred and they evolved into modern-day man.

Evolutionary theory has its roots in the ancient Greek philosophers who contributed a materialistic mindset to every field of human knowledge. Greek thought has been responsible for the rational and logical Western mindset. They used a methodology of questions and answers when considering the origins of the universe, our human values, and our identity, explaining natural phenomena on scientific grounds, and arrived at conclusions about such principles as the atomic composition of matter and its classification into elements.

Thales (640–550 BC) identified water as the fundamental source of all things. Leucippus (440 BC) and Democritus (429 BC) determined the atom is the basic substance for the composition of the universe and all things. He believed our souls are composed of atoms, thought itself was a physical process, and the universe had no supernatural intervention.[1] Lucretius Carus (95–55 BC) said there is no place for a supernatural dimension with an intervening deity; everything obeyed the inexorable laws of chance and nature.[2] The rationale behind Darwin's theory of evolution is intimately related to the prevailing historical belief system at the time of its conception.

The prevailing views among Greek thinkers, later adopted by Romans, and into the Middle Ages, inevitably led to the development of differing views on the creation of the universe and life. Nicolas Copernicus (AD 1479–1543) challenged the earth-centered, orthodox view of the Roman Catholic Church.

It became evident through Galileo (AD 1564–1642) that geocentricism was in error. That led to warfare between science and theology in the Roman Catholic Church.

The discovery of the laws of the universe made a big impact on the beginning of modern science, socialism, and secular humanism. This period was noted by a humanistic revival expressed in art and literature. A number of intellectually disciplined thinkers came on the scene, such as Francis Bacon (1561–1626), Rene Descartes (1596–1650), Francis Marie Voltaire, and Jean Jacques Rousseau (1712–1778). They challenged the teaching of the Roman church on the doctrine of creation. During the eighteenth and nineteenth centuries, the French Revolution and the Industrial Revolution of England brought tremendous changes in every field.

There were key people who laid the basis for atheism and materialistic modern evolution. Comte de Buffon (1707–1788) proposed the mutability of species in relation to changes in environment. Buffon sowed the seeds of the idea of atheistic evolution, and these later grew in the minds of his successors. James Hutton (1726–1797), who advanced the idea of an evolutionary earth formation, set the stage for Charles Lyell's study and the views of Jean-Baptiste Larmark (1744–1829). Next came Charles Darwin (1803–82), who proposed a theory of evolution based on natural selection in his treatise, *On the Origin of Species*.

Darwin explained the mysteries of the origin of all things from a natural perspective. His theory said life began as a simple organism and evolved into more complex organisms, which implies an intelligent directing force, but avoided any inference to the supernatural.[3] This theory of origin was satisfying to people looking for an escape from religious dogma. Christianity was then also declining in intellectual circles as people began to place more confidence in science. The theory of evolution gradually replaced creation in the field of academics. The anti-God spirit was now unmasked.

Chapter Twelve

The Way to Overcome the Challenge

A Theory of Emptiness

WITH THE GROWING erosion in man's values due to the misuse of knowledge in science and technology, we need to reexamine the decline of ethical values. This downward pattern came from the wrong thinking based on materialism that denies the existence of God.

Henry Morris says, "The whole area of the behavior sciences today is thoroughly dominated by its humanism, and this has resulted in incalculable harm."[1] He continues, "Experiments with monkeys or other animals (even with insects) are used for guidance in dealing with human problems."[2] Under this system, it is assumed that man is simply an evolved animal and his wrongdoings have been evaluated as animalistic.

According to the Bible, man has not evolved from other material or life forms but was created with a spirit (soul) in the image of God. Henry Morris points out an interesting and clear contradiction, about the word "psychology," which means "study of the soul," as modern psychologists do not even believe in the soul.[3] Under this framework, no one can be accused of wrongdoing for behavioral reasons. This idea is dangerous enough to destroy the basic moral fabric of our society. If we are only animals, then society must tolerate people acting like animals.

The evolutionary idea cannot bring eternal hope or ultimate value. Its application brings about harmful influences. This crisis in values is not merely one of many problems facing today's global pattern, it is at the core of all issues. It causes a lack of respect and a spirit of selfishness.

Evolutionists point to the fossil records as evidence. The big question here is of evidence. If their idea is correct, we should have an orderly, accurate progression with layer-by-layer fossils. But evidence does not connect the ladder of living organisms with clear intermediary forms, including people. Evolutionists have manipulated the ladder of materials according to their assumptions. To this day, no scientist has been able to reproduce the tremendous change between animal and human life. Granted, there are similarities between different kinds of creatures.

The evidence given by evolutionists that human beings evolved from lower types of animals is derived from uncertain observations. The similarity of the fossil findings of humans or animals used to prove human beings first existed in such forms don't give us the exact evidence for justifying these claims. Their diagrammed pictures of the creature's progressive development do not present any convincing evidence.

David D. Riegle says when the first fossil bones were discovered many years ago, there were no other bones with which to compare them, no other measurements by which to judge them, so the first drawings of ancient men were the products of imagination. Those who drew the first pictures imagined man as rather ape-like in appearance, so they drew him with the facial features halfway between a man and an ape. They gave him a slightly crouching stance, a long face with huge jaws, and a look of doubtful intelligence.[4]

Evolution is a groundless theory that does not have evidence that human beings evolved from lower life forms. It seems to be a made-up, imaginary theory. Evolution cannot explain the nature of human soul and spirit at all, as that is an intangible area. The only source of explanation of the intangible spirit and soul of human beings is the creation community.

God created human beings in His image. Man's spirit is a part of God's image and likeness. Similarly, we find there is a remarkable likeness in internal body systems, embryos, and skeletons of some creatures in relation to people. Their likeness would seem to justify the evolutionists' position that humans evolved. We have to consider these similarities are not based on evolution, but instead are designed by a Creator, and manifest a consistent characteristic. Professor Leonard Sweet says:

> We are a part of nature. Just look at our DNA. All of nature is a part of us in that genetic endowment. The fruit fly (Drosophilia melanogater) shares about 50% of its DNA with humans. In other words flies are 50% of the way to being human. Chimpanzees share about 97% of their DNA with humans. The human body is one of the natural wonders of the world . . . What a difference that 3% makes.[5]

As Creator, God can easily make distinctions in His creation. If we believe we are purposeful beings created by God, then we should have a different view of life than those who believe we are accidents. According to the theory of evolution, only the fittest and strongest survive. This idea brings about dangerous results to our world. It means physically or mentally challenged people don't have any value at all. The elderly or the sick serve no purpose other than to be preyed upon by those who are young and healthy. The Christian worldview rejects such ridiculous notions. Consider these questions:

1. Where did the very first matter come from?
2. Where and how did the first life come into being?
3. How do you know that people are an ultimate by-product?
4. Where did human conscience come from and how did it evolve?
5. Where does one species end and another begin?
6. How have human intelligence and spirit developed?
7. Which species evolved into the ape?
8. Where did the first man and woman come from?
9. How could they have evolved into both male and female?
10. Why does it take a female and a male to create a single offspring?
11. Where do space and time come from?
12. Why does the earth have only enough oxygen for life to survive?
13. Where did gravity come from?
14. Why do the forces of gravity and electricity have the powers that they do? Did they evolve? If so, how?
15. Why do people live only on earth?
16. Why and how does the earth revolve around the sun?
17. Why do people look for God?
18. Why do animals have a pair of eyes and ears, and one nose, and one mouth?
19. Why does the tall fruit tree produce small fruit while the small fruit tree produces big fruit?

The evolutionary idea cannot easily explain why the nine planets in the solar system, including the earth, need constant rotation in reference to their revolution around the sun, and why Venus rotates slowly backward. Evolutionists have no "how and why" answers to the intricacies of the body, such as our vision. Geoffrey Simmons, a medical doctor, says, "Eyelids blink to protect our eyes. Eyeballs roll up at night to protect them from injury when not being used. Tears bring oxygen to the cornea, carry chemicals that kill bacteria and proteins to coat the eyes, wash the eyes, and move debris toward a lower drain, or lacrimal duct.[6]

Evolution only raises new questions that cannot be answered about the origin of the universe and life. In order for accidental chance to be the origin of life, reproductive living ingredients must be collectively gathered, and meet in the same location at the same time with tremendous accuracy. Can we imagine these highly accurate conditions and orderly arrangements could be possible by accidental chance? These arrangements or conditions could not bring about the scientifically perfect system of conditions that are precisely interrelated and interdependent toward a goal.

An accidental chance means it is only a chance, much like a lottery ticket. It isn't systematically correct, planned, or purposeful. Regarding the system of DNA, Stephen C. Meyer, a philosopher, says, "Our experience with information-intensive systems (especially codes and languages) indicates that such systems always come from an intelligent source—i.e., from mental or personal agents, not chance or material necessity."[7]

Jonathan Wells, a biologist, says, "DNA mutations never alter the endpoint of embryonic development; they cannot even change the species, and the evidence for the natural selection has been discredited, and the relevance of industrial melanism to evolution is in doubt."[8]

Cornelius Hunter, a scientist, says life cell machinery uses the genetic code to interpret the information stored in the DNA molecule when creating proteins, making use of the same code, not following accidental blind chance.[9] This means the function of the life cell is not dependent upon accidental chance, but depends upon a perfect, systemically planned regularity.

If accidental chance evolves, then presumably the cycle of life would eventually stop. The end point for atheistic evolution, therefore, is a meaningless and purposeless human existence. But we know better than that. The theory of accidental chance by mutation or natural selection has been found to be statistically impossible, and does not make any sense at all. All evidences confirm that an intelligent Creator, the God of the Bible, designed and created the universe and all living things.

Right Choice

We must remove any confusion about the origin of all things. The Bible clearly indicates God created all things. The exceptional variations in the world came from partially disharmonious nature rooted in the result of man's sinful nature and his abuses for his selfishness. Consider 1 Corinthians 15:38-39: "God gives it a body as he has determined, and to each kind of seed he gives its own body. Not all flesh is the same: People have one kind of flesh, animals have another, birds another and fish another." Therefore, we cannot accept evolution as a scientifically and ultimately true explanation.

Evolution does not have a clear explanation about the origin of the universe and life, or of sin and death. It depends upon hypothetical evidences that are willfully obstinate toward God and His created works. What advantage and benefits are there in being a follower of the theory of evolution? This theory is tremendously harmful for human life. Behind it there is only a purposeful evil spirit who is against God. We must not become victims of this spirit.

Chapter Thirteen

A World of Confusion and Struggle

AS I LOOK back on my childhood days, I am filled with nostalgia when I remember smiling children playing in the street, good relationships among neighbors, and unlocked doors without the concern of danger. There was great serenity around us, like a kind of paradise. I long for those days, because it seems to me a paradise is now lost.

Many are now barricaded behind walls of wariness, fear, and mistrust. Desperate events take place in our communities. Our traditional values are threatened by radical revisions. Value systems today hold materialism alone is the ultimate reality. Moral values have become relative, focused on individual and collective selfishness, without a guiding certainty.

Global

The twentieth century turned out to be most destructive in history with its ideas and political fanaticism—Nazism and Communism—which are rooted in racism. Dictators like Hitler, the supreme evolutionist, and Nazism are the ultimate fruit of the evolutionary tree.[1] Stalin who cruelly oppressed hundreds of millions of people used survival of the fittest based on evolution as an excuse for his evil practices and lust for political power.

These ideas gave people an excuse for the unimaginable mistreatment of people and brought unspeakable harm to the world. In World War I there were more than 8,500,000 fatalities in the armies involved. In World War II there were over 56,125,262 soldiers and civilians killed between 1939 and 1945, and millions died in concentration camps.[2] As an example of the use of chemical weapons in WW I, it is estimated that 125,000 tons of chemical weapons were used by all sides. Mustard gas alone killed 91,000 and injured 1.2 million.[3]

These tragic actions are rooted in the harmful influences of evolutionary humanism. The progress of science brought a feeling of boundless optimism and hope for peace in the world. But, through exalting the power of human reason, it has shaped man to be rational, selfish, cold, arrogant, and inhuman.

Most world societies have been built on a religious foundation. Uniquely, the Western world has been rooted in the Christian worldview. This worldview has been declining in intellectual circles by the influence of materialism and evolutionary thought. This has produced a harmful confusion, and undesirable influences on life—in religion, ideology, society, and family structures. Not only is life viewed and explained in a materialistic way, human interaction has become more and more impersonal. This satisfies people who are looking for an escape from religious thought and morality, as it looks at the world through the eye of science.

People in the Western world are turning away from a Christian worldview and the God of the Bible. The result is a loss of respect for God, even a loss of belief in His existence, a strongly negative attitude towards divine authority and Christianity, the dignity of man, and morality, traditional family structure, and other anti-religious ideas.

The theory of evolution has gradually replaced biblical creation in the field of academics.[4] Joseph S. Nye, Jr., professor at Harvard's Kennedy School of Government says, "The United States is not alone in many of the cultural changes that cause controversy in developed countries. Respect for authority and some standards of behavior have declined since 1960 throughout the western world."[5]

We are today facing the greatest threat to our stability in the history of mankind—attacks involving weapons of mass destruction—nuclear, biological, or chemical. Because of the unimaginable power of nuclear weapons and their ability to destroy large parts of the earth, this is an ongoing threat for our existence.

Martin Schram says the world has 32,000 nuclear bombs and warheads that are the property of just eight nations—the United States, Russia, Britain, France, China, Israel, India and Pakistan. All but 2,000 of them belong to the United States and Russia. Only a few know what it is like to actually have a finger on the nuclear button, and bear the burden for making the decision as to whether millions, perhaps billions, will live or die.[6] Today, some countries like Iran and North Korea are trying to develop nuclear bombs.

Ongoing conflicts are taking place in the Middle East, Africa and some parts of South Asia. Evil terrorist attacks are shaking the world's security. We can never forget the tragic attack in New York by Islamic terrorists on September 11, 2001.

Despite outstanding achievements for our everyday convenience, there are many unwanted and dangerous by-products of the rapid growth of technology. Nuclear weapons with mass-killing capabilities, and dangerous chemical products for destroying life are being produced in the name of defense or attack purposes. As nuclear technology spreads, terrorists attempt to acquire and use atomic weapons for their ends. As long as atomic bombs exist, the nuclear threat will never stop and continues to be a nightmare for all of us.

Tension and fear is caused by the threat of worldwide destruction through nuclear war, and ecological disasters. The danger of nuclear fallout from explosions or reactor spills brings about related problems for our global food production and health, and the potential contamination of our air, land, and water. Toxic chemicals, synthetic food additives, and pesticides cause harmful diseases. The earth is experiencing calamities such as drought, floods, polluted air, water shortages, weather changes and the like.

The empire-building self-glorification of man, combined with a lack of the fear of God, has resulted in a diminishing of human dignity. Around the world sinful behavior is multiplying—falsehoods, deceits, extreme selfishness, cruelty, immorality, violence, rage, dissensions, factions, and the like. The world seems to be surely approaching to its final days, just as the predictions of the Bible have told us in Matthew 24:3-11.

Local

Evolutionary materialism and postmodernism are causing our local societies, formerly based on a traditional Christian worldview, to rapidly decline. This has resulted in detrimental moral effects: an increasing crime rate, drug and alcohol abuse, and domestic violence. Local societies face social and cultural conflicts, political and religious differences, social collective issues, gun violence, and a seemingly irreparable threat of terrorism and nuclear war.

Joseph S. Nye Jr. points out that culture wars could adversely affect American power if citizens become so distracted or divided by domestic battles over social and cultural issues that the United States loses the capacity to act collectively in foreign policy.[7] We also face tremendous challenges from ongoing natural and man-made disasters: hurricanes, bird flu, the MRSA virus, Zika virus, rising numbers of earthquakes, drought, wars, and terrorism.

There are numerous warnings of social disintegration as our society falls into extreme materialism. The nuclear family has given way to the undesirable single-parent family. Today's parents focus on earning higher incomes to enjoy a better standard of living. As a result, children often do not receive close care and attention under adequate supervision. Without a daily close relationship of a stable family, children and the younger generation grow up in a spiritual vacuum where the highest value of life is placed on money and the acquisition of material possessions. Disturbed juveniles may be increasingly vulnerable to drug abuse, violent activities, and promiscuous acts.

Our children and young people are being exposed to dangerous situations. They have become victims to drug abuse, abortion, violent crime, broken homes, severe depression and frustration, increased alcoholism, suicide, learning disabilities and behavioral disorders, and sexual abuse. This applies, of course, to adults too. Youth are dying on the streets or on school campuses by gun violence. Today's kids are desensitized to violence as never before.

In the field of education, emphasis is not on the forming of good personalities and character. Chris Hedges says elite universities disdain honest intellectual inquiry, are distrustful of authority, fiercely independent, and often subversive. Most universities no longer hire the best and most experienced teachers.[8] Jay Stracker says, "Millions of young people are hiding behind a chemical curtain of drugs, and millions more are drowning in a sea of alcohol, and today, however, these problems are spreading at epidemic portions in the middle schools and senior high schools and colleges."[9] All these negative things are plunging family values established on a biblical worldview into danger.

Rapid technological progress and evolutionary materialism have led people to selfishness, greed, and disgraceful behavior. Chris Hedges says, "America, the country of my birth, the country that formed and shaped me, the country of my father, my father's father, stretching back to the generations of my family that were here for the country's founding, is so diminished as to be unrecognizable." He adds, "Our nation has been hijacked by oligarchs, corporations, and a narrow, selfish, political, and economic elite, a small and privileged group that governs, and often steals, on behalf of moneyed interests.[10] Hedges goes on to say, "The corporation is designed to make money without regard to human life, the social good, or the impact of the corporation's activities on the environment. Corporations by law impose a legal duty on corporate executives to make the largest profits possible for shareholders."[11]

Where did this endlessly selfish spirit come from? It comes from the invisible influence and force of evil. Confusion and struggles will always with us, no matter how hard we try to do the best. In the societies of our world, love, grace, and forgiveness are not found, only cruelty.

Reasons for Confusion and Struggles

Throughout human history people have recognized the evil among us, and in many cases perpetrated it. This world is not getting better and better. The evil that was passed on to us has had tremendous impact upon our daily lives. Even Jesus Christ called Satan the ruler of the world (John 12:31, 16:11). The earth is Satan's playground. He is gifted with high intelligence (Gen. 3) and greater power than humans (Matt. 4:1-10; Luke 10:18; Rom. 16:20; Rev. 12:7). The fundamental reason for confusion and struggles come from the work of Satan and from lives without God. Therefore, unless there is a fundamental change in our mentality and spiritual condition, we will continue to become encapsulated in a world of confusion and struggles and live a life without guidance for the future.

Chapter Fourteen

Current Struggles of the Church

The True Nature of the Church

THE CHURCH BEGAN with Christ's resurrection and is the body and bride of Christ, and the earthly kingdom community of God. Its worldwide purpose in the last days is a salvation mission (John 17:14-21; Acts 1:8). Christ is head over everything for the church (Eph. 1:22; Col. 1:20; Rev. 21:5). He is her "current divine purpose."[1] Christ provided the church with resurrection life (Rom. 4:24; Col. 3:1-3). The church is waiting for the coming of the Bridegroom (Christ) and will be joined to Christ after He returns to this world (Matt. 25:1-13); 2 Cor. 11:2; Rev. 19:7-9). As God's earthly mission representatives we must strive for holiness (sanctification) through the Holy Spirit. (See 1 Cor. 3:17; 2 Cor. 13:5.) The goal of believers should be to restore the nature and spirit of the early apostolic church who met for communion and prayer and reached out to the world with the gospel of Jesus Christ (Acts 2:42-46; Acts 8:4).

Struggles of the Church

The church today faces challenges from the secular mindset. As materialism and humanism affects biblically-based values, secular society is increasingly experiencing corruption, violence, an anti-God spirit, and abuses. People now focus on the acquisition of material goods and the enjoyment of physical pleasure. Christian values are being eroded and a rise of rebellion against the God of the Bible is taking place. Unfortunately, even some Christian leaders reject the claims that Jesus Christ is the Son of God and the Bible is the inerrant, inspired Word of God.

The growing decline of Christian influence in our society is accelerating instability and slowly dividing our society. Without the correcting, guiding certainty of faith, our society is losing a clear sense of spiritual and moral direction, and its responsibility. This causes us to lose hope. The more our society eliminates God and the Bible, the more we will lose our place as a global role model.

To restore and rebuild our long-established Christian foundations we must have biblical discernment. Then we will be aware of the true hope that God promises and the value of life in Christ. The world cannot give us meaning for life, or hope for tomorrow. It only offers confusing, impersonal, dehumanizing, inhumane, and harmful ways of thinking.

We must not forget evil is behind spiritual conflict, confusion, and the loss of a spirit of integrity. The Bible tells us to "be alert" as the devil is on the prowl (1 Peter 5:8–9). We must keep the Word of God in mind and pray to receive the power of the Holy Spirit to defeat the temptations of evil. Christ is one who gives us strength (Phil. 4:13).

Reasons for Decline

Confusion comes to those who have neglected or discarded the long- and well-established wisdom of the Word of God. The

Bible says confusion comes from the "god of this age" (2 Cor. 4:4), gives birth to wrong choices, and brings about decline.

The decline of the church can be traced to a loss of true faith, and following the pattern of the world systems, rather than fully depending upon God's authority. The Bible warns that "falling away" from the true faith in Christ will characterize the decline of the church during the days prior to Christ's second coming to the world. Therefore, true believers should not be confused and surprised at this; it shows the return of our Lord is getting closer.

There are various sources for the decline of the church. First, there is a tremendous lack of deep, meaningful spiritual messages on the cross of Jesus Christ: why He came in human flesh; how He was without sin; why He died on the cross; and what the resurrection means.

Second, the interpretation of the gospel of Christ is based on the secular mind, fundamentally ignoring the credibility of the Bible as the historical record of inspired authors, the teachings of the disciples, the historicity of Christ, and His coming return.

Third, Christian leaders have turned to worldly wisdom and values. Part of the church has fallen into secularism and proclaims man is basically good, no one will be lost, and man's salvation does not depend only on Jesus Christ. Instead of the believer's prayer and the leading of the Holy Spirit, they employ worldly wisdom.

Fourth, the source of decline comes evangelical secularism. These churches stand on the foundation of biblical authority, but also on politics and money, rather than sincere prayer and dependence upon the power of the Holy Spirit.

Fifth, decline comes from a lack of teaching on repentance, Christ's return, and a true eternal hope in Christ. They teach various ways to achieve success in life, even by adopting corrupting, immoral ways as an option. These evangelical churches are compromised by secularism. For their survival, they adopt the world's techniques and wisdom.

So the decline of the church is rooted in the influence of science and technology, humanistic rationalism, materialism, and evolutionary thought.

Lastly, it seems the curtain of God's salvation plan for Gentiles is slowly being lowered. That means the satisfactory number of Gentile believers in Christ is reaching its full count. According to the Bible, the current age is the end-time period of human history, the last opportunity for salvation for the human race. The opportunity for salvation through faith in Jesus Christ will not be forever, and is approaching the end. God's salvation plan for mankind will not transform the whole human race and establish Christian nations on earth. Only those who accept Christ Jesus as their Savior are born into the eternal kingdom of God (John 6:37, 39, 44; 13:18; 14:1–3; Acts15:14).

Israel rejected God's grace and His salvation offer and crucified Christ on the cross. As a result, God rejected them. They lost their country for almost two thousand years until their national restoration. Paul says if God did not spare Israel, "He will not spare you either" (Rom. 11: 21). Human history will end up with God's eternal judgment (2 Peter 3:7–12)

The reasons for the decline of the church are spiritual warning signs to the present world. Christians should carefully listen to the true voice of God. To be spiritually ready, we must follow what the Bible says and live holy lives. The world will not pay attention to a Spiritless church that is losing its integrity, spiritual passion, power, the practice of prayer, and strong evangelism (Matt. 24:18–20).

Trends

Today's trends are increasingly eroding traditional values. Even Christmas celebrations, which are deeply rooted in our culture, are facing a crisis. Some have a mission to try to erase the symbols of Christmas—and even the use of the greeting "Merry

Christmas." This is a cultural collision between well-established traditional and cultural values and the values based on today's rising flag of diversity.

Western civilization has had around 2,000 years of history. This nation has been built for 240 years on the foundation of a Christian cultural heritage. Every country has its own history, tradition, and culture expressed by its own religious attitude and forms that must not be erased.

The three national holidays of Easter, Christmas, and Thanksgiving Day are rooted in our Christian faith and history. No matter how this nation has been modernized and diversified, the day of celebrating the birth of Jesus Christ should not be changed into a "winter festival." No matter how much some campaign to get rid of Christmas symbols, they cannot erase the facts of Christmas Day's standing in our tradition, culture, and history. Just as we cannot erase our own birthdays, so we cannot erase our Lord's birthday, either. We Christians must stand up for the glory of God and the true faith of Jesus Christ more than ever before.

Chapter Fifteen

Roots and Branches

THE TERM "ROOTS and branches" generally portrays a mosaic of a father and a mother, and either a child, or children as a basic family unit: in other words, a small social unit. Healthy roots produce healthy branches that bear healthy fruit. Parents who are healthy spiritually, mentally, and emotionally produce healthy children. Their children, as loving and beautiful branches with good character, will have positive futures. We were born to be loved in a family, and born to love the family of God. This will produce a healthy society and nation.

Where Does Family Begin?

Scripture says God "created man in his own image" (Gen. 1:27). Genesis 2:24 says, "That is why a man leaves his father and mother and is united to his wife, and they become one flesh."

The family unit as the very first social unit is based on a man and a woman. The genuine character of a family is strengthened when we submit to one another out reverence for Christ. Husbands are to love their wives just as Christ loves the church. The wife must respect her husband (Eph. 5:26–33). This is God's timeless wisdom. The husband and the wife make a beautiful team and can have a harmonious spiritual relationship under God. Both of their duties involve giving, and not just receiving. The successful married life should not include any impurity between the husband and wife. Marriage is a spiritual union as well as a physical, mental, and emotional one. In other words, the family is a sacred small church for the glory of God.

Disintegrating Roots

Human beings are relational beings designed by God for a relation life. Family life is to be built on the spirit of love, trust, honesty, purity, and union with one another in God. Love is the basic ingredient in human life. The happiness of family members comes out of loving one another. The loving relationship of parents is the root of happiness of the family members.

A bad relationship due to dishonesty in the family produces tragedy. Dishonesty begins small and then enslaves, as a clean conscience is lost. Dishonest behavior breaks up families, bringing many problems both directly and indirectly. Dishonesty grows like environmental pollution. The family bond will go from love to hatred, from trust to doubt and distrust, from unity to disunity, from respect to contempt, from joy to sadness, and from hope to despair. Dishonesty and impurity in family life can never bring about peace and love, only destruction and disintegration.

The family is an earthly mission for the kingdom's sake. One of the primary reasons is the challenging task of caring for, nurturing, and training children under God's wisdom. The roles of a mother or father are very important in raising godly offspring who seek to be a blessing to their family and to society.

For these tasks, parents must be equipped with loving, faithful, positive mindsets. As parents, our responsibilities to our children are far more important than anything else we could do. If parents (roots) have problems the children (branches) will inherit problems as side effects.

Our postmodern, materialistic society, and no-God mindset, has a negative influence on our families. As a result, people lose love, and respect toward one another. Many are ambivalent about having children as they did not experience loving relationships in their homes. Individual selfishness will result without warm and loving relationships.

Family relationships are showing serious signs of disintegration as the increase of broken families reaches epidemic proportions.[1] Love, warmth, honesty, and security are necessary for a healthy family union, as well as a sense of belonging among family members. Dr. Appel says, "Family problems are caused by fragmentation in the family, and a lack of communication.[2]

A son asked his father, "Dad, could you play with me?"

"I am busy now. Later I will."

Whenever his son asked his dad to play with him he'd say, "Later. I'll play later."

The son grew up. Now when the father wants to spend time with his grown-up son, the son says, "I'm busy right now, can I talk to you later?"

Communication is crucial. As a tree with shallow roots cannot withstand stormy winds, immature and unbalanced parents cannot maintain healthy and happy families. Only healthy and growing roots produce healthy branches. Everyone prefers good news to sad, smiles to frowns, encouragement to criticism, happiness to unhappiness, harmony to disharmony.

Healthy Roots for Healthy Branches

It's common sense that healthy roots make healthy branches. Healthy families are key for our society and nation. So parents must be healthy, supportive, and harmonious one with another.

We are not perfect; all of us were damaged by sin. We all need helpful guidance. Our sin nature causes us to wear a mask to hide the emotions below the surface.

There are some helpful guidelines for getting along with family members.

Florence Littauer says, "By looking at our inborn desires, our underlying needs and our repressed emotions, our eyes will be open and we will be open and we will obtain, perhaps for the first time, some insight about who really are. There is no magic wand to transform us into angels, but as we look at ourselves as God created us to be and come before Him in honesty, He will touch us with His healing power."[3] We can start with discovering the real us so we can be healthy and harmonious family members. Larry Crabb points out, "We need deep longings in the human heart for relationship and impact rather than personal needs for security and significance."[4]

For the restoration of fractured and broken homes and shattered marriages, we must recognize God created us in His image. We are not by-products of accidental chance. But God's image in us was terribly crushed and we lost our identity, because of the fall of Adam. God is our source; He alone will fill our deep longings and make us healthy parents. Only God alone can quench our thirsty hearts and restore the family spirit.

Healthy parents are balanced spiritually, mentality, and emotionally within God's boundaries. In order for healthy parents to make healthy branches, they must allow the grace of God to flood in. We are to love the Lord with all hearts and minds, and our neighbors as ourselves (Matt. 22:37-39). The Bible also says God will "turn the hearts of the parents to their children, and the hearts of children to their parents" (Mal. 4:6). Family integrity depends on the perfect God of love and justice. We are to love the Lord sincerely; love ourselves, and our neighbors; teach the young diligently (Deut. 6:7-9), and live by His Word (Deut. 6:8).

Living in integrity in the family for the glory of God will avoid ruin and moral crises. Integrity can be sweetly built through consistent discipline of our longings, and practicing loving one another. Positive ingredients for healthy families are: encouragement, prayer, serving, kindness, understanding, smiles, sharing the concerns of the family, forgiveness, and spending time together.

God is our power source for the family. The apostle Paul said, "I can do all this through him who gives me strength" (Phil. 4:13). He is our source for a loving and positive mindset. When the roots and branches have a true, faithful relationship with God, the result will be healthy and happy families. John the apostle says, "Dear friend, I pray that you may enjoy good health and that all may go well with you, even as your soul is getting along well" (3 John 1:2). God's grace for the undeserving is shown in His Son's substitutional death on the cross to save us from our sins and give us eternal life.

God is the source of the true love that produces a harmonious family spirit. I have personally experienced how hearty, loving, and warm words between my wife and me can dramatically make a difference. The Bible says, "A gentle answer turns away wrath, but a harsh word stirs up anger" (Prov. 15:1). The fragrance of heartfelt, loving talk results in loving responses and calms emotional pain. Plant loving words and attitudes into family members and the family environment will change. As Ralph Waldo Emerson put it: "Love is our highest word and synonym for God."[5] Wayne W. Dyer says, "Love is cooperation rather than competition."[6]

True love cannot come from us, but by our connection with Jesus Christ. Parents must have a sincere and faithful relationship with God. They must love His Word, practice what it says, and teach His Word to their children.

Our quiet and shy granddaughter, Rebecca, loved us, but she did not voluntarily greet us when we'd visit. I'd say, "I love you

Rebecca." Then I'd ask, "Do you know how much Grandma and Grandpa love you?" When we'd visit, I'd honk the car horn as my visiting signal in front of her house. One day a great change came when Rebecca flew out of her house, hugged me, and blew a kiss to my cheek, and with a happy smile said, "Hi, Papa, I love you . . . I missed you." Rebecca changed into an expressive young girl. Whenever I see her, I hold her hands, and pray for her and for her future. Her smiling face is like angel's and is imprinted as a beautiful picture on my heart.

Philip Yancy tells this story.

> Not long ago I heard from a pastor friend who was battling with his fifteen-year old daughter. He knew she was using birth control, and several nights she had not bothered to come home at all. The parents had tried various forms of punishment, to no avail. The daughter lied to them, deceived them, and found a way to turn the tables on them: "It's your fault for being so strict!" My friend told me, "I remember standing before the plate-glass window in my living room, staring out into the darkness, waiting for her to come home. I wanted to be like the father of the Prodigal son, yet I was furious with my daughter for the way she would manipulate us and twist the knife to hurt us. And of course, she was hurting more than anyone . . . And yet I must tell you, when my daughter came home that night, or rather the next morning, I wanted nothing in the world so much as to take her in my arms, to love her, to tell her I wanted the best for her. I was a helpless, lovesick father.[7]

Deep wounds can be healed and relationship restored on both sides. This is our story and can be your story, too. A father or mother who speaks in a warm and loving way so the child feels the love of parent will remove fear and calm down sadness and anger. Love is personal and produces great hope and joy.

No one can destroy the power of love in the world because it belongs to God's image and character.

As long as children see in their parents something of the image of the parents' love reflected, they will have hope and peace in their minds. An image of God's love and justice and grace reflected in us proves we are created by Him. Do not underestimate the power of God's love. Chris Hedges says, "Love constantly rises up to remind a wayward society of what is real and what is illusion."[8]

The news media show us enough of human cruelty and disgrace in the world every day. But we have seen the power of grace and love as the hungry are fed, the weak helped, and the needy provided for in the name of Jesus Christ. The power of love and grace are strong.

The world is full of fakes pretending to be genuine. It is hard to determine if something is real or not, so we are often deceived by imitations. Fakes come out of an illusive desire, and are full of vanity, but will eventually be discovered. God designed truth to win over lies. Our conscience is the last fortress for the image of God in us. It is a wonderful gift that allows us to see what is right and what is not right. Let's not allow our consciences to be blinded. Evil cannot destroy it, but we can be deceived so we do not see the truth. Do not get along with evil. God does not set the boundary lines of truth to be broken down. We need the guidelines of the Bible and the wisdom of discernment to deal with the fakes and the corruption of this world.

Our ultimate guidelines are found in reading the Word of God and in prayer. No matter how difficult personal relationships are in this sinful world, we will find wisdom for healthy family lives, and learn how to avoid the devil's temptation. God's Word helps our attitudes and thinking processes. We should take it in daily, the same way we eat food daily.

The darkness of evil cannot crush the power and the grace and love of God in Christ (2 Cor. 4:8–10). The image of God's love and grace reflected in us cannot be erased.

Chapter Sixteen

Restoration of God's Boundaries

AS WE WALKED in a small park near our house, an unfamiliar woman smiled at me and my wife. Naturally, we smiled back and waved. She had given us a joyful morning gift. Warm hearts cannot be taught in a classroom. A natural and warm smile comes from a warm and encouraging spirit. When life is lived within God's boundaries, warmth is restored to our hearts.

Awareness of Boundaries

Everywhere we turn there are boundaries in our lives we should be aware of. Earth, our grand home site, is a boundary for all human life and living creatures. We humans have many visible and invisible boundaries in our lives—spiritually, intellectually, emotionally, and physically. Crossing these boundaries causes problems and severe struggles.

In the biblical sense, the Hebrew word *kebel* in Psalm 16:5–6 is translated into a "boundary" in English literally meaning "a rope, and a measuring line."[1] Human life has a boundary. God the Creator set His created world to consist of a boundary line as a set limit.

Creation had meaning and purpose. If the boundaries of a system are divided, or working against each another, they really are not part of a system at all. These boundaries clearly guide us to better lives for God's glory. (See Ps. 16:5–6).

Awareness of God's Laws

Generally, man thinks of freedom as being unencumbered by boundaries. In order to function well and avoid problems, regulations are required. God wants humans to enjoy maximized freedom *within* His boundaries. While we humans live a limited life under natural laws, our freedoms are maximized within God's boundaries. Boundaries are set so people can live a happy life.

Discipline with obedience is needed to comply with God's laws. I have seen the results of my granddaughter's ice-skating practice and hard training under wonderful coaches, which has led to beautiful performances on the ice and awards. Harold Kushner says, "It is only by subjecting oneself to rigorous discipline, as the musician or the athlete does, that we gain the ability to do demanding and impressive things."[2] God gives His laws to us so we can learn how to live in this world and avoid tragedy.

Being obedient to God leads us to freely dedicate ourselves to God's will and control bad desires stirred by evil, rather than allowing them to rule us. Adam's disobedience brought serious problems into his life and the lives of his descendants—death and a disharmony that causes natural disasters on earth (Gen. 3:17; Job 1:15-20).

Henry Cloud and John Townsend say, "Boundaries define us. They define what is me and what is not me. A boundary shows me where I end and someone else begins, leading me to a sense of ownership."[3] Boundaries require that man must do his part for a safe and better life, and for a good relationship between man and God.

God sets limits and wants man to respect His authority. He promises blessings in return (Deut. 28:1–2). We need to accept and follow God's ways for peaceful, wise, and prosperous lives. It is arrogant to ignore God's authority. If we wish to live a life of blessing, we must learn from the example of the people of Israel who met tremendous hardships throughout history. Israel's history on earth surely proves God is deeply involved in our lives in purposeful ways.

Man lives a life as a limited creature and cannot survive without God's grace. No matter how we try to ignore God's authority, it is impossible for us to escape His boundaries. God's spiritual and moral boundaries are designed for a better life. If we stay within His boundaries, we will have joyful lives because God is the source of truth, love, joy, and justice.

Experiencing God's Strength by Practicing His Word

Knowing about God's spiritual and moral laws is one thing, but experiencing His strength when we practice His Word and pray, is another. In our sinful natures we can't keep God's law well. That is why God came into this world in human flesh and died a sacrificial death on the cross. To live a holy life as a Christian, our dreams and desires must comply with God's boundary laws.

The laws of the world are not eternal but temporal; they are not perfect because imperfect humans made them. Only God's law and His grace are constant and eternal. The God of the Bible, as the true source of love and justice, expects His authority and regulations to be respected. He wants to see His image reflected in us. We must not try to test God's special grace, love, and patience. If we keep His boundary laws we will reap eternal blessing.

Chapter Seventeen

The Fragrance of Grace

A Blanket of Grace

EVEN IN THE turmoil of the world, we can sense the fragrance of God around us. The literal Greek word for grace is the "divine influence upon the heart and its reflection in the life," and "favor," and "joy" and "thanks."[1] There are two meanings of grace. There is the gracefulness of a person in acts, speech, words, and deed. Then there is grace on the part of a giver and the feeling of gratitude on the part of the receiver.

There is also "blanket grace." With their softness and flexibility, blankets have multiple uses, and are used for wrapping. When we have good relationships with others, it is as if a blanket of grace is wrapped around them.

Jesus had that blanket of grace to embrace the sick, the blind, widowers, children, tax collectors, demon-possessed people, the rich and poor, women and men, Jews and Gentiles. He broke down the walls of man's sinful prejudice, and displayed God's special grace as His loving, fragrant character. Jesus showed the most beautiful fragrance of God's grace and heart in His love to the world.

Jesus told the parable of the prodigal son (Luke 15), a story of loss and the excitement of rediscovery that ends with joy. The return of the lost son made his father much happier than always having a son with him at home. The father did not punish the son. The joy of finding the one who was lost shows us how God's grace wraps around us as a blanket. Jesus says, "There will be more rejoicing in heaven over one sinner who repents" (Luke 15:7). God is still waiting for all to come to Him in repentance before the appointed end of time.

The ultimate fragrance of grace was demonstrated by Jesus' death on the cross. In His last words spoken in painful agony on the cross, He said, "Father, forgive them, for they do not know what they are doing" (Luke 23:34). God's loving "blanket heart" was shown to the world through Jesus Christ. But the privilege of salvation as God's ultimate grace will be applied only to those who accept Christ as their personal Savior. This grace is received both from God the Father (2 Cor. 1:12) and from Christ (Gal. 1:6; Rom. 5:15). Jesus Christ is the true Son of God; He holds all authority in heaven and on earth. Do not let the deceptive powers of Satan devour you. Take off the wrappings of hypocrisy and evil, and overcome temptation.

God does not ask what kinds of sin we have committed, but He wants us to acknowledge we are sinners. Our sins can only be forgiven by accepting His son Jesus Christ as our Savior. He wants to see His own image restored in us. Jesus Christ invites us to come to Him and rest (Matt. 11:28-30). This is made possible through the cross. In Christ we can receive a "blanket heart" to be witnesses to the world.

God's Image Reflected

The earth is filled with various fragrances of God's free blessings and grace. Many people do not recognize these as God's free blessings to those who do not deserve them. Instead they destroy and abuse the grace of God. The pattern of this destructive influence spreads out like a stormy wind. However, the fragrance of grace as a reflection of God's own image still appears all around us.

In a crusade in Korea on June 3, 1973, Billy Graham told what took place on Heartbreak Ridge as twelve American soldiers huddled in the cold around Christmas time. An enemy sneaked through the line and threw a hand grenade into the middle of them. One soldier jumped on top of it, and pulled it to his heart before it exploded. He died, but his friends were saved. He accepted the attack of the evil in his own body to save his friends and paid the price with his life.

John Newton (1725–1807) was a troublemaker, and lived a corrupt life in his youth. But the book, *The Imitation of Christ* by Thomas Kempis, guided him to God's grace. The chains of his corrupt life were broken. He went from being a slave trader to a preacher of Jesus Christ. He went from being lost to being found.

A new believer named Helen received a wonderful fragrance of God's grace. Her pilgrimage had been marked by confusion, disappointment, wanderings, detours, betrayal, and dead ends. There was a conflict between her and her son and her business was shaky. When a close friend asked for some financial help she made an interest-free personal loan that did not end well.

All the discord with her son, business, and friendship confused Helen. She backed away from her newfound faith and neglected church for a time. After over a year of wandering, she prayed, "Where and how can I go to find your grace?" She put all her cares and burdens upon the Lord Jesus Christ with her whole heart and an amazing peace and grace filled her heart.

Her heart was filled with thanksgiving toward the Lord. She and her son reconciled, and her business was reestablished. She had received a great gift of the grace of God, breaking the pressures of worry. She and her son now live a joyful and positive life and are full of passion to help the needy. She now understands God works all things to the good for those who are seeking Him.

When I got cancer I turned my heart toward the Lord and thanked Him because it made me come much closer to Him. I put my life in the Lord's hands. After surgery on July 26, 2010, my recovery was faster than expected. I noticed God's grace and love anew, and found it to be very personal. Cancer taught me to find who I am and to sincerely search for His grace and healing. I experienced that God is the one who helps those who seeks His help by faith.

On December 25, 2012 my wife, Mary, and I were joyfully singing "Angels We Have Heard on High." All of sudden I experienced the power of the Holy Spirit; I was moved and burst into tears as I realized Jesus Christ is the Most High beyond my imagination. As a sinner, I did not deserve to call on His name. I sensed His deep love for me, and my heart was filled with that love. I knew my identity is found in Him. His name is the greatest in the universe!

It is hard to express God's grace in human words. This experience started me on the process of writing this book for His glory. As I look back on my own spiritual pilgrimage, I see it was marked by healing miracles of grace. I can't help but proclaim the powerful warm grace of Jesus Christ. The Spirit of my Lord fills me with His grace, joy, and hope, and gives me new eyes to notice His work in my life. He is truly the living God and the source of grace for all. I felt a new understanding of who God is and how much he loves us.

Worldly values cannot affect those who experience the true love and grace of Christ. God's grace comes freely to those who do not deserve it, to those who accept Jesus Christ, the true source of grace and forgiveness, as their personal Savior.

Our role is to praise Him until His return to this world as the greatest King of kings and Judge of all.

From the sacrifices of missionaries, we learn what is the most valuable thing in life. They are Christ's earthly mission agents so unbelievers can find eternal life in Christ. They choose suffering for Christ rather than following their own comfort. Because of the love of Christ, they choose to carry out the Great Commission of Christ (Matt. 28:18-20). They pay the price by their sufferings and sacrifices to offer the good news of Jesus Christ.

Chapter Eighteen

Man's Last Revolt Against His Creator

The First Humanism

THE BEGINNING OF Godless humanism began with Nimrod who founded the city of Babylon. He and his followers became the first collective group of humanists by their open rebellion against God. They came together in pride to raise up their names and conquer the whole earth.

Humanism is the rational study of man's dignity and value for bettering man's condition *without God*. Scientific knowledge and methods are regarded as the most reliable source, and man is considered capable of self-fulfillment. Science is seen as explaining reality for a new world; God is nonexistent; the earth came out evolutionary random chance; trusting self is the key to success; good and evil are relative; guilt, blame, anger, and pain are essential steps to the social transformation process; life has no purpose; self is the most important; there is no fixed order.

Stepping into the Domain of God's Authority

The current worldwide situations of unrest and crisis are final signs of the end times. Change due to the new technology has been so rapid that we are losing our sense of direction. Using information technologies and knowledge, man is attempting to transcend his biological limitations and go beyond the limits of his genetic legacy. Through the study of artificial intelligence, cyborgs, and genetic engineering, man is trying to acquire everlasting life by conquering aging and death, which belong to God's domain. Artificial intelligence technology is the ability of an artificial mechanism to display intelligent functions like the human brain by the use of computers. It has been already applied in vehicles, navigation, service, medical, therapeutic, and manufacturing.

Today we are facing the age of robots with machines capable of carrying out a complex series of automatic actions the way people do, which may be a huge threat to our future. Georgia Tech has an online class led by an artificial intelligence instructor. A leading law firm has hired a robot as an attorney. Wall Street is using robots in financial analysis, according to *The New York Times*. Yuval Harari, professor at Hebrew University, says artificial intelligence will take many jobs away from people. It may not be possible for today's children to prepare for their lives with knowledge obtained from their parents and teachers. Dr. Hanson of Hanson Robotics who developed a human-like android, "Sophia," said, "Twenty years from now I believe human-like robots like this will walk among us. I think that artificial intelligence will evolve to the point where they will truly be our friends."[1]

Biological engineering technology is deeply involved in much of the food industry. Yuval Harari says, "Biological engineering is a deliberate human intervention on the biological level (e.g. implanting a gene) aimed at modifying an organism's shape, capabilities, needs or desires; geneticists do not only want to transform living lineages and aim to revive extinct creatures as well. Genetic engineering and other forms of biological engineering might enable us to make far-reaching alterations not only to our physiology, immune systems, and life expectancy, but also to our intellectual and emotional capacities."[2]

Harari defines cyborgs as "beings that combine organic and inorganic parts, such as a humans with bionic hands." He says, "We stand poised on the brink of becoming true cyborgs, of having inorganic features that are inseparable from our bodies, features that modify our abilities, desires, personalities and identities; and Sapiens, too, are being turned into cyborgs."[3] Harari continues, "The Defense Advanced Research Projects Agency is developing cyborgs out of insects. The idea is to implant electronic chips, detectors and processors in the body of a fly or cockroach, which will enable either a human or an automatic operator to control the insect's movements remotely and to absorb and transmit information. Such a fly could be sitting on the wall at enemy headquarters, eavesdrop on the most secret conversation, and if it isn't caught first by a spider, could inform us exactly what the enemy is planning."[4]

Many fear that "doomsday" technologies will put an end to human history. Particularly, many deep thinkers fear today's advanced chemical, biological and nuclear weapons based on new technologies could fall into the hands of dangerous individuals for bad purposes, producing nightmare scenarios.

This frightening prospect is possible because of man's sinful nature and selfishness, and would affect our destiny. Man's ambition and arrogant pride has already caused him to step into the domain of the Creator's authority. He is attempting to conquer death by developing super-humans through genetic and cyborg technologies.

Technology has already begun creating gaps between the younger and older generation in obtaining knowledge, and wider gaps between the rich and poor. This dramatic change is causing people to change their patterns of behavior. Man's immoderate curiosity and challenging of his given limits and boundaries are like the actions of the biblical Nimrod.

Concluding Remarks

In this age of scientific revolution, our world includes artificial intelligence, biological and genetic engineering technologies, and manipulation through experimental processes that may extend our lives beyond our imagination. New technologies encourage our dependence upon them. According to Yuval Harari, "Genetic engineering and other forms of biological engineering might enable us to make far-reaching alterations not only to our physiology, immune system and life expectancy, but also to our intellectual and emotional capacities. And there seems to be no insurmountable technical barrier preventing us from producing super-humans."[5]

We already see today's various genetically-modified food manipulated by man's design. It seems evolutionary scientists believe they can perpetuate life, and produce superhuman beings through artificially selecting desirable genetic qualities and eliminating undesirable qualities. This is like waiting for the appearance of the devil, and is a dangerous practice.

Man's present genetic biological changes are not caused by natural selection, but are products of a creator, and man's selection and manipulation. Accordingly, Darwinian evolutionary theory is totally absurd and, ironically, is locked into a contradictory concept. These changes by artificial, genetic, and cyborg engineering technologies prove that the universe and life were created by the Creator.

Robots with artificial intelligence are made by man and can only be imitations of humans. Man's uniqueness, his morality, creativity, religious sense, feelings, expressions, artistic capacity, are all given by God and cannot be copied. Robots are only machines that follow man's manipulations. Even though successful cyborgs are built by biological engineering technologies, they are not perfect and eternal because imperfect man built them.

Many are falling for the illusion they can conquer the power of death. They are eager to step into the domain of God's authority. Their efforts cannot come true, rather they prove there is an eternal life beyond us. Under the system of evolutionary ideas, materialism, and atheism, man does not have a meaningful and valuable future, and no eternal life. Without God he is bound to his animal inclinations.

We are created by God's love and grace and are very valuable to God. We are in His ultimate control and live in His appointed boundaries. Only the Maker of the universe knows our life course. The Creator is the originator of our existence and is our controller. Unless we seek Him, we will live a dark, wandering life and forever be a lost one. We need to open our spiritual eyes to see God's grace all around us. We don't deserve these things, but they are free of charge. The Giver of life, who is the Maker of the universe and life, has paid the cost by giving up His Son on the cross so we can have eternal life in Him.

Chapter Nineteen

Thirsty for a Powerful World Leader

WITH THE RAPIDLY growing erosion in today's morality, spirituality, and interpersonal values, this present age is moving toward the final round of history. The worldwide decline of the certainty of biblical faith is causing society to go in a wrong direction. In Europe churches are increasingly empty and the churchgoing population is graying. Many churches are falling away from biblical faith. Jesus asked, "When the Son of Man comes, will he find faith on the earth?" (Luke 18:8).

Today many believe science explains reality; materialism is absolute; God is nonexistent; the earth come out of evolutionary random chance; trusting self is the key to success; good and evil are relative; and guilt, blame, anger, and pain are essential steps to the social transformation process. Our traditional beliefs are no longer valid to many and have almost disappeared. The influence of the church upon the world is rapidly declining as the church compromises with the world.

Because of the rapid changes, wars, and natural disasters, people are falling into confusion and becoming concerned only for their physical survival, and not the impending disasters such as a nuclear holocaust, or cultural, and religious conflicts.

Setting the Stage for the Antichrist

Fearful situations are pushing the world to look for hope for tomorrow in a powerful world leader who would provide security, and solve our complex problems. These expectations seem to be preparing the world for the coming of the Antichrist who is Satan's earthly agent.

The Bible tells us of the coming appearance of the Antichrist at the end of the age, before Christ's return. (See Matt. 24:3-7, 11-14, 22; Matt. 24:40-42; Luke 19:8; 2 Thess. 2:14, 7:12; 2 Tim. 3:1-5; and 2 Tim. 4:3-4; and Rev. 13.) The time is approaching when he is to dramatically appear on the scene, but no one knows the exact time of his appearance. This will be a real man and the final sign of the end times. The anti-God spirit, supported by Satan, is actively working in the world and paving the way for coming of the Antichrist (2 Thess. 2:3).

Who is the Antichrist?

After believers are caught up in the clouds to meet the Lord in the air (1 Thess. 4:15-17), the Antichrist comes on the scene. The word "Antichrist" appears only in John's epistles (1 John 2:18, 22; 4:3; 2 John 7) in a singular form and "antichrists" in the plural form. John description is anyone who denies that denies Jesus is the Christ (1 John 2:22); anyone who denies the Father and Son (1 John 2:23); every spirit that does not acknowledge Jesus is not from God (1 John 4:3); those who do not acknowledge Jesus Christ as coming in the flesh (2 John 7).

The prefix "anti" in Greek means "against" or "opposite" or "opposed to." It can also mean "instead of" or "in the place of" or "a substitute for." The Antichrist will oppose Christ while pretending to be a good person and an angel of light in order to deceive (2 Thess. 2:1-10).

This masquerade will convince the world to accept him as its new world leader. John, the apostle, said antichrists as forerunners of Satan have been acting in the world since the first man. But the Antichrist of the future will be the head of the world system in the last day of the last days, before the return of Jesus Christ. Jesus said, "I am come in my Father's name, and ye receive me not: if another shall come in his own name, him ye will receive" (John 5:43 KJV). This "another" must be an individual, the Antichrist. New Testament scholar, Bob Gundry, defines this man as "*serious* Antichrist, *the* Antichrist."[1]

According to the Bible, his appearance as the earthly mission agent of Satan will come with "power through signs and wonders that serve the lie" (2 Thess. 2:9-10). The Antichrist will not only one be against Christ but will also want to take the place of Christ. He will promise a golden future, and appear as a wonderful "angel of light" before taking control of the world.

Satan's servants masquerade as "servants of righteousness" and fake spiritual workers (2 Cor. 11:14-15; Eph. 2:1-2). Satan is behind today's crises, increasing crime, drugs, and sexual immorality.

Two lines have been present in human history: the line of Christ beginning with Adam, and the line of the anti-God and the Antichrist that begins with Cain. The main goal of the Antichrist and Satan is to destroy the work of God and to make people fall away from God, or not accept Christ. Do you belong to Christ or the Satan?

The Titles of the Antichrist

Besides his title as the Antichrist, this man will also be known as the son of perdition, man of lawlessness, and the lawless one (2 John 1:7, 20; 2 Thess. 2:3, 8), and the beast (Rev. 13:1, 10).

The Bible declares that the Antichrist is a liar becaus
is Satan, the father of lies (John 8:44). He will be marked
the beginning to end by deceit and lies. Daniel 7:8, 23–25 speaks
of the Antichrist as the "little horn."

The Antichrist will come in the midst of unprecedented
local and global crises with hidden dark plans to deceive the
world for his kingdom of darkness. The world that longs for a
great world leader who will resolve many complicated problems
will easily accept his cunningly false and persuasive leadership.

His Dark Empire

The Antichrist will be made the head of a world system with
strong enmity against God (Rev. 13, 16:13–14). There will be
world unity in the political, economic, and religious systems. He
will be the world's last dictator, empowered directly by Satan, and
helped by the false prophet for his dark plan. The inhabitants of
the world will worship him (Rev. 13:18). All will be forced to
receive a mark on the right hand or forehead, or killed if they
refuse to worship his image (Rev. 16–18). No one on earth will
be able to buy or sell unless he has the mark, which is the "name
of the beast" or the "number of his name" (Rev. 13:17). The
beast's number is 666, the number of man.

Grant R. Jeffrey explains the number of the beast as follows:
"The Greek text does not spell out the number as we do in
English, but rather it uses the three Greek letters that convey
the number 666. The Bible does not actually claim that 666 is
the actual mark, though it is possible. This man's name in the
Greek or Hebrew language will be equivalent numerically to
the number 666."[2]

Today's technology makes this possible. We experience laser
scanners at supermarkets, department stores that record items
we purchase, and we pay for our purchases with credit or debit
cards. Today's various computerized surveillance systems record

our daily activities. The technology in biochips and biometrics will make data collection of our daily movements possible. Spy satellites will be our watchdogs. The Antichrist will use technology as a "Beast ID." Through technology, the whole world will be well organized and centralized for the Antichrist to exercise an absolute control over politics, finances, and religion. The Antichrist will act like a world savior and will perform miraculous signs. He'll gather the leaders of the whole world together for battle (Rev. 16:14).

When the Antichrist comes to take all power, he will severely persecute, conquer, and rule true believers in Christ (Rev. 13:7) who are left on the earth. The prophet Amos said the Lord reveals His plan to His servants (Amos 3:7). Jesus said the Holy Spirit will teach us, and remind us of His words (John 14:26), and will guide us into "all truth," and tell us "what is to come" (John 16:13).

True believers who are guided by the Spirit of God will avoid the great sufferings caused by the Antichrist on the earth. Believers who do not turn away from Christ will undergo temporary suffering. Most of all people on earth will worship the beast (the Antichrist). This period of the Antichrist' reign will be called the great tribulation and it will be an unspeakably terrible time. Those who want to enter the kingdom of heaven, should accept Christ as their Savior now. This day is the best opportunity to experience the grace of God in Christ.

The Hope of Ultimate Restoration

THE WORLD TODAY does not give us a bright vision for now and the future. The Bible indicates mankind has been bound to confusion and suffering by the power of the devil because of the fall of Adam. Is there then any hope for ultimate restoration?

Yes. The Bible says Christ, who defeated the power of death, will gloriously return to this world. We will experience a perfect restoration through Jesus Christ (Titus 2:13). Only Jesus Christ is the answer.

Why doesn't Christ come back to save the world right away? God does not work according to man's expectation, but according to His appointed timing. Just as we have choices, so God does too. God is waiting for the full number of His people to come back to Him (John 6:39-40).

Believers must look forward to the day of Christ's soon coming. That day will bring about the destruction of the heavens by fire, and the elements will melt in the heat. But, in keeping with His promise, we are looking forward to a new heaven and a new earth (2 Peter 3:12-13). The Lord's return is our ultimate hope.

Wisdom and Discernment through the Spirit of God

The Bible warns us the sinful world is running toward inevitable collapse. As believers, we must walk in the will of God, in His Word, and receive the Holy Spirit. The Spirit, who is called the "Spirit of truth" will guide us into all truth and tell us what is yet to come (John 16:13; 1 Cor. 2:10). The biblical word "truth" in the Greek word means primarily, "unconcealed, manifest, conforming to reality and true to fact, and taking off the confusion." Thus, in Jesus Christ there is no confusion, but only the truth.[1]

Only those who accept Christ as Savior can receive the Spirit of God (John 15:26). We should ask God for wisdom, who gives generously to all without finding fault (James 1:5-6). Today we should be Christ's witnesses to the unbelievers.

Yes, we must still work hard for a living. The Bible says, "The one who is unwilling to work shall not eat" (2 Thess. 3:10). Where your mind is, there is your priority. In order to reach unbelievers, believers should live faithfully with integrity as true Christians. The people of the world are thirsty for finding out what is real. The Holy Spirit will give us wisdom and discernment and help us understand the deceptive work of the devil.

A Healthy Understanding of Christ's Return

Christ's return is the source of ultimate hope for mankind. To understand the prophecy concerning Christ's return to this world, we should observe the spiritual attitudes and conditions before the first coming of Jesus Christ.

Jewish religious leaders in Jesus' time believed the biblical prophecies concerning the Messiah. They believed the Messiah would be born in Bethlehem (Micah 5:2), and that He would suffer as foretold in Isaiah 53. But they expected the Messiah to be a great military and political savior who would set national Israel free from the Roman Empire. They made their interpretations based on their present situation. Ironically, only a few wise men and shepherds were aware of His birth.

Furthermore, these same religious leaders became His greatest enemies. When the Messiah for whom they had been waiting finally came, they didn't recognize Him (Matt. 2:6). Even when Christ came on the scene and performed supernatural miracles, Israel rejected Him and crucified Him on the cross. They were spiritually corrupt, bound to political strategies and just waited passively for the Messiah.

We now have the reliable and steadfast guidelines of the Bible that gives us a good understanding of Christ's second coming so we can be prepared.

Chapter Twenty-One

The Question of Suffering

WHY DO INNOCENT people suffer? Some consider suffering to be God's punishment, and some think of it as a warning sign of what might lie ahead. Can God be good and still allow suffering?

The Atheistic View

The atheist says if God created everything, and if everything He created is good, then He must be the cause of suffering. But even atheists see that argument as being inconsistent with who God might be (if, from their point of view, He actually exists). Instead, they see suffering as chance, and a consequence of the evolutionary process.

The Christian View

The Christian worldview says suffering is the direct result of disobedience to God. The Bible tells us creation is cursed because of man's violation of God's law (Gen. 3:17–18). The entire creation has been groaning as in childbirth right up to the present time (Rom. 8:21–22). Our sinful behaviors have destructive consequences that are passed on to the rest of creation.

Romans 5:12 says, "Therefore, just as sin entered the world through one man, and death through sin, and in this way death came to all people, because all sinned" (Rom. 5:12). The sinful DNA nature of humans has been passed on to all.

Suffering can also be a test of our faith. Just look at Job's life. He was a righteous man who lost everything through no fault of his own. Satan asked to sift Job and God gave him permission. In a sense, Job suffered for his faith. This made his suffering a privilege.

Other Causes

Not all suffering comes directly from God. The Creator limits Himself in what He can and cannot do in His creation, just as He cannot tell a lie. The laws of nature are precise, highly reliable, and always work the same way. If we do not comply with the system of gravity, it might be the cause of some suffering. Falling is based on the power of gravity. The laws of nature treat everyone alike. Sometimes suffering is caused by the carelessness of people, or wrong and greedy desires. Airplanes crash; so do automobiles. All calamities have their own reasons; we can't always know or understand what those reasons are.

Nobody likes pain, but it is not always bad. Pain in our bodies can be a sign something is wrong. When we touch something hot, we feel pain to make us jerk our hand away before we are seriously burned. If we could not feel pain, our lives would be faced with danger.

In some cases, we should see pain as positive. Ludwig Van Beethoven grew up with an alcoholic father. His family was poor so he went to work at eleven years of age. His mother died when he was seventeen. As a thirty-year old pianist and composer, he lost his hearing. He was in despair, but did not lose his passion for music. He kept studying and composed his famous ninth symphony, among many other pieces. Beethoven found great meaning in his suffering. His greatness came not from good conditions, but from making the best of bad conditions.

This means our attitudes during times of suffering are very important. There is truth we need to know in suffering: we can learn from it. Suffering brings patience, and through it often an unspeakable treasure. God gives us strength, patience, and hope as He renews our spiritual resources when we run dry. Suffering isn't incompatible with the character of a loving God; God can and does achieve His purposes through painful suffering. Suffering restrains us, keeps us from committing evil, makes us humble, reminds us of our weakness, and drives us to God. God promises all things will work together for good for those who love Him and are called according to His purposes (Rom. 8:28).

A Right Understanding of God's Wrath

The difficult issues of the "whys" of evil and suffering in the world have been stumbling blocks for many throughout history. How does God, who is always love, permit evil and suffering? What about God's wrath? The Christian worldview tends to emphasize God's love and grace more than His justice, but this is not a complete approach. The Bible says God is a personal being. Hebrews 11:6 says, "Without faith it is impossible to please God, because anyone who comes to him must believe that he exists and that he rewards those who earnestly seek him." Yet atheists and many liberal minds reject this and attempt to prove God does not exist. They say it is unreasonable or irrational to believe He exists. In response to the claims of atheists, the Bible clearly speaks of the root of evil things and suffering as the products of both men and evil together.

If there is no law in our society, there is no punishment for crime. The law has two sides: one is protection for lawkeepers, the other is wrath for the lawbreaker. Justice requires wrath. Thus, we must know that the law exists for justice and righteousness, and deals with sin by punishing the lawbreaker. That is why all nations have their own system of laws in order to punish evildoers for their lawbreaking, and for the protection of lawkeepers, and national security and safety.

In the same manner, just as we cannot mix light and darkness, God's holy character cannot be mixed with human sin. God's justice was partially exercised after the fall of Adam; and his descendants now have death and suffering as a punishment as God left them to do what they want. (See Rom. 1:28–31.)

God warns us that His final wrath will be given from heaven against all ungodliness and unrighteous of men who don't retain the knowledge of God. God gives corrupt people over to the sinful desires of their hearts to do what they want until His ultimate plan is done. Suffering in the world is a present sign of God's partial wrath (judgment) against unrighteousness and ungodliness.

What benefit do people get from refusing Jesus Christ as their Savior? The God of justice sent His Son to this sinful world to offer salvation. He poured His wrath out over His sinless Son to save those who accept Christ as their Savior. Many stumble at this concept of the wrath of God. They only want to hear beautiful music, a bright message, and think of Christ as a friend or helper who can understand them. This is true, but we also have to pay attention to what the Bible shows us about God's true character being both love and justice. In order to justify their sins, many reject God's existence and His authority. If God had no justice with wrath, we could not believe His love and the promise of His blessing either.

The sufferings in the world reveal God is righteous and holy. God's true grace was shown to the world when He gave up His

Son to free us from the grip of our sinful past and from eternal judgment. God put Himself on our side.

Why do parents have wrath against the evildoing of their children? It is because they love their children and want them to live right. Parents who cannot rebuke their children for wrongdoings are not good parents. We should not complain against God about the sufferings in the world. God's grace is everywhere around us and comes freely to us who do not deserve it. God allows the sunlight and moonlight to rise on the bad and the good, and sends clouds, rain, and snow on the faithful and the unfaithful. God provides what we need through what He has created (Matt. 6:26).

Paul the apostle went from being the persecutor to the persecuted under serious persecution and sufferings. His life and the lives of many other early Christians were kept strong by their faith in Christ (Phil. 4:13; 2 Cor. 4:8–10). Many Christians have been tortured and killed for their faith. The Bible speaks about this in Hebrews 11:35-38 saying, "The world was not worthy of them." Why do missionaries proclaim the message of Jesus Christ under hardship and persecution and give up careers to serve God? Because Christ defeated the power of the death and proved He is the Son of God.

Those who suffer for Christ know obeying Him is much more valuable than anything in the world, because they have received the power and strength of the Holy Spirit (1 Cor. 1:27). Wherever they preach the gospel of Christ, a better life in every area results—schools for Christian purposes, civil liberties, hospitals, and so on.

God's gifts are not contingent upon our hard work to earn them. The offer of God's grace still extends to undeserving humans until His return to this world. We need to stop ignoring the authority of God and just breathe in the pure grace of Jesus Christ. The fear of the Lord is the best gift of God for us (Prov. 1:7).

Chapter Twenty-Two

Final Reflections

IT IS EVIDENT the world is rapidly changing. We humans are easily shaken and broken by problems without a hopeful alternative. We seem unable to prevent the endless natural disasters, tragedies, problems, hatreds, and abuses we see every day. We see and hear the chaotic voices of the march toward doomsday and feel the very real threat of extinction.

Many focus on materialism and pleasure seeking, instead of being filled with faith. Society is becoming increasingly inhuman, more abusive, and lacking in respect. Moral values are relative, and no longer based on biblical values. Wise leaders are lacking. Unimaginable selfishness sits in the hearts of people. Secular public opinions are placed above what the Bible says. Many are rapidly chasing after meaning, purpose, and truth in all the wrong places. We no longer live in a predominantly Christian culture based on the standards of the Bible. While these issues are nothing new, we are now reaching an unprecedented crisis stage.

The dehumanizing inventions of high-tech systems cause the pride of man to rise up against God. Leonard Sweet says, "Spirituality is shaped by technology."[1] Evil is destroying the structure of family. We are living in rapidly changing times with thinking, values, and living patterns all moving in an ungodly direction. This is a time of extreme spiritual warfare between God's goodness and Satan's evil. All these signs have to do with Christ's second coming (Luke 18:8; Luke 21:28).

Jesus said there would be four different kinds of listeners to the message of kingdom of God in the last days: those who had the message snatched away by the evil one, those who fall away after persecution, those have the message choked out because of the worries of life and their wealth, and those who hear and understand the message (Matt. 13:19-26).

What is influencing your life now? Judgment must begin with the house of God (1 Peter 4:17). We are told to be "self-controlled, and alert," as the devil is looking for those he can "devour." We are to resist him, and stand firm in the faith (1 Peter 5:8-9).

The faithful family must be salt and light to the world until Christ's return, restoring the image of God. Some are backsliding from the grace of God and chasing after the trends of the world. Jesus said, "For many are invited, but few are chosen" (Matt. 22:14). John A. Sanford says, "Those who do enter the kingdom are those who have come to recognize the reality of the inner world and to respond to its demands upon them for consciousness."[2]

Encouragement for a Life Lived in Fullness

Why is there so much negativity in this world? Why does every living thing come to its termination, including our lives? This present world is not permanent. The confused and corrupted conditions of the world came after Adam and Eve's sin. Their sin not only caused confusion, decay, death, degeneration and destruction, but also their sinful DNA was passed on to their descendants. We are all now subject to death and suffering until Christ returns and the new heaven and earth comes.

The world is now in bondage to this confusion, decay, corruption, and death. No matter how beautiful the physical world looks, the fate of man and the fate of the world are moving toward their termination. D. M. Lloyd-Jones gives us a good explanation for this tragic event: "Everything has been reduced from an original state of perfection to its present state and condition."[3] According to the Bible, this present world is not as it was, nor as it was meant to be.

But there is good news for us. We can be saved and restored as God's children from this tragic bondage of Satan. Our acceptance of Christ will bring His fullness of grace, joy, and love into our lives.

The temptation of evil exists all around. We are told not to allow room for Satan to get in. For a successful Christian life we should follow what Psalms 1:1 says, "Blessed is the one who does not walk in step with the wicked or stand in the way that sinners take or sit in the company of mockers."

Our hope is in Jesus Christ who breaks the bondage of evil. In Christ we can overcome negative thoughts, and habitual sins. We are not to be deceived by the devil's temptations or controlled by negative thoughts and habits. Satan tries to keep us from realizing who we are and what our relationship is in Christ. But, when we accept Christ as our Lord, we belong to His kingdom and are God's children. Satan cannot knock us down and rob us of our spiritual freedom through his accusations, deception, and control any more. Be free in the name of Jesus Christ. True Christians are earnestly expecting our Lord's return to this world. This age is a grace period for man's salvation. Don't miss the message of the endless grace of God in Jesus Christ.

Peter and Paul are examples of God's grace to the undeserving. Peter thought he would never betray Christ, but he fell hard. After he betrayed Christ, he repented. Christ forgave Peter and treated him with wonderful grace. Peter was filled with the Holy Spirit, was fully renewed, and set free from his guilt. Paul, who formerly persecuted Christians, encountered the living Christ. He became an unprecedented missionary, and an apostle to the world. God's grace made Peter and Paul deserving for the kingdom of God.

The full grace of Christ appears to those who, aware of their sin and shame, and thirsty for an inner joy, turn to Christ. God is waiting for those who will seek Him before the close of the grace period of salvation.

The grace of Christ will never let us down. It is the key to living our best life with eternity in view. Are you still in doubt about the love of God in Christ? He is waiting for you now. This will make all the difference for where you will spend eternity. We cannot do anything about our past mistakes, but today we can make a decision to come to Jesus Christ who guarantees our eternal life and give us full joy.

Build your life on the eternal, unshakable foundation of Jesus Christ!

Notes

Chapter 1: A Wonderful and Intelligent Designer

1. Arthur F. Glasser, *The Word Among Us*, (Nashville: Word Publishing, 1989), 34.
2. Howard A. Snyder, *Earthcurrents: The Struggle for the World's Soul* (Nashville: Abingdon Press, 1995), 264.
3. James W. Sire, *The Universe Next Door* (Downers Grove: InterVarsity Press, 2009), 36–37.
4. John Bright, *The Kingdom of God* (New York: Abingdon-Cokesbury, 1953), 30.
5. Snyder, 264.
6. Neil Broom, *How Blind is the Watchmaker?* (Downers Grove: InterVarsity Press, 2001), 46–47.
7. William Demski, *Intelligent Design* (Downers Grove: InterVarsity Press, 1999), 98.
8. Snyder, 252.
9. *Webster's Dictionary of the English Language Unabridged-Encyclopedia Edition* (New York: Publishers International Press, n.d.).

10. Paul Davis, "The Unreasonable Effectiveness of Science," in *Evidence of Purpose,* John Templeton, ed. (New York: Continuum, 1994), 45.

11. Hugh Ross, *The Fingerprint of God* (Orange: Promise Publishing Co., 1989), 120.

12. Ibid., 127.

13. Geoffrey Simmons, *What Darwin Didn't Know* (Eugene: Harvest House Publishers, 2004), 53.

14. Ibid., 151.

15. Philip Yancey and Paul Brand, *Fearfully and Wonderfully Made* (Grand Rapids: Zondervan, 1980), 151.

16. Ibid., 151.

17. Simmons, 163.

18. Simmons, 221.

19. Yancey and Brand, 163–164.

20. Werner Gitt, "Design by Information" in *The Big Argument: Does God Exist?,* John Ashton and Michael Westacott (Green Forest: Master Books, 2005), 51.

21. Danny R. Faulkner, "Design by Information: *in The Big Argument: Does God Exist?,* John Ashton and Michael Westacott (Green Forest: Master Books, 2005), 27.

Chapter 2: The Divinely Inspired Bible

1. Irving L. Jensen, *Survey of the New Testament* (Chicago: Moody Press, 1981), 15.

2. Wayne Grudem, *Systematic Theology* (Grand Rapids: Zondervan Publishing House, 1994), 47.

3. C. W. Slemming, *The Bible Digest* (Grand Rapids: Kregel Publications, 1960), 16.

4. Ibid., 16.

5. Paul E. Little, *Know Why You Believe* (Downers Grove: InterVarsity, 2000), 87.

6. Mark W. Chavalas and K. Lawson Younger, Jr., *Mesopotamia and the Bible* (Grand Rapids: Baker Academic, 2002), 35.

7. Ibid., 172.

8. Alfred Hoerth and John McRay, *Bible Archaeology* (Grand Rapids: Baker Books, 2005), 106.

9. Paul Ferguson, "The Historical Reliability of the Old Testament" in *The Big Argument: Does God Exist?*, John Ashton and Michael Westcott (Green Forest: Master Books, 2006), 274.

10. Ibid., 275.

11. Ibid., 284–286.

12. David K. Dowcon, "Archaeological Evidence for the Exodus," *The Big Argument*, 268.

13. J. Barton Payne, *Encyclopedia of Biblical Prophecy* (Grand Rapids: Baker House, 1973), 681.

Chapter 4: Understanding Satan's Character and Goal

1. Lewis S. Chafer, *Systematic Theology* (Wheaton: Victor Books, 1988), 360.

2. Don Uhm, *The Signs and Involvements of God* (Enumclaw: WinePress Publishing, 2009), 22.

Chapter 5: The Completion of Creation

1. Wayne Grudem, *Systematic Theology* (Grand Rapids: Zondervan, 1994), 442.

2. Sire, 29.

3. Grudem, 443.

4. Millard J. Erickson, *Christian Theology* (Grand Rapids: Baker Book House, 1985), 428.

Chapter 7: The Beginning of the End Times

1. Charles Ryrie, *Basic Theology* (Wheaton: Victor Books, 1995), 286.

2. Philip Yancey, *What's So Amazing About Grace* (Grand Rapids: Zondervan, 1997), 70.

Chapter 8: Defeating the Power of Death

1. Ralph O. Muncaster, *A Skeptic's Search For God* (Eugene: Harvest House Publishers, 2002), 219.
2. Ibid., 203.
3. Philip Schaff, *History of the Christian Church* (Grand Rapids: Eerdmans Publishing, vol. 2, 1985), 637-639.
4. Josh MacDowell, *Evidence for Christianity* (Nashville: Thomas Nelson, 2006), 185.
5. Schaff, vol. 2, 47.
6. Ibid., 653-655.
7. Andrew Miller, *Miller's Church History* (Addison: Bible Truth Publishers, 1980), 179.
8. Josh MacDowell, *Evidence for Christianity*, 186.
9. Schaff, vol. 2, 709.
10. Ibid., 709.
11. Ibid., 664-665.
12. Andrew Miller, 165.
13. Flavius Josephus, *The Complete Works of Josephus* (Grand Rapids: Kregel Publications, 1999), 988.
14. John Ashton and Michael Westcott, *The Big Argument: Does God Exist?* (Master Books, 2006), 362.
15. Josh MacDowell, *A Ready Defense* (Nashville: Thomas Nelson, 1990), 198.
16. Muncaster, 218.
17. Ibid., 218.
18. *The New Westminster Dictionary of the Bible*, ed. William Demski and James M. Kushner (Grand Rapids: Brazos Press, 2001), 115.

Chapter 9: The Consequences of Rejection of Jesus Christ

1. Grudem, 853-859, 864.
2. Grant R. Jeffrey, *Surveillance Society* (Toronto: Frontier Research Publications, Inc., 2000), 208.
3. Uhm, 70.

Chapter 11: The Unmasked Power on the Scene

1. Morton Donner, Kenneth E. Eble, and Robert E. Hebling, *The Intellectual Tradition of the West*, vol. 1 (Glenview: Scott, Foresman and Company, 1967), 50.
2. Ian Y. Taylor, *In the Minds of Men* (Toronto: TEE Publishing, 1987), 11.
3. Ibid., 159.

Chapter 12: The Way to Overcome the Challenge

1. Henry Morris, *The Long War Against God* (Green Forest: Master Books, 2003), 32–36.
2. Ibid., 32.
3. Ibid., 33.
4. David D. Riegle, *Creation or Evolution?* (Grand Rapids: Zondervan Publishing House, 1972), 66.
5. Leonard Sweet, *Carpe Mañana: Is Your Church Ready to Seize Tomorrow?* (Grand Rapids: Zondervan, 2001), 160.
6. Simmons, 55.
7. Stephen C. Meyer, "Word Games: DNA, Design and Intelligence," in *Signs of Intelligence: Understanding Intelligent Design*, William Demski and James Kushiner, eds. (Grand Rapids: Brazo Press, 2001), 115.
8. William Demski, Jonathan Wells, and William S. Harris, *The Design of Life: Discovering Signs of Intelligence in Biological Systems,* 2008 (Seattle: Discovery Institute Press), 123.
9. Cornelius G. Hunter, *Darwin's God* (Grand Rapids: Grand Rapids Press, 2001) 24.

Chapter 13: A World of Confusion and Struggle

1. Morris, 75.
2. *Encyclopedia Britannica.*
3. Martin Schram, *Avoiding Armageddon* (New York: Basic Books, 2003), 127.
4. Uhm, 42.
5. Nye, Jr., 74.

6. Schram, 15.
7. Joseph S. Nye Jr., in *Storming Toward Armageddon: Essays in Apocalypse,* David Breese, Tim LaHaye, Texe Marrs, David A. Lewis (Green Forest: New Leaf Press, 1993), 48.
8. Chris Hedge, *Empire of Illusion,* (Nashville: Thomas Nelson Publishers, 2009), 89, 110.
9. Jay Strack, *Drugs and Drinking: What Every Teen and Parent Should Know* (Nashville: Thomas Nelson Publishers, 1985), 9.
10. Hedges, 142.
11. Ibid., 162.

Chapter 14: The Current Struggles of the Church

1. Lewis S. Chafer, *Systematic Theology,* vol. 2 (Wheaton: Victor Books, 1988), 237.

Chapter 15: Roots and Branches

1. George Sweeting, *Special Sermons* (Chicago: Moody Press, 1985), 305.
2. Ibid., 342.
3. Florence Littauer, *Your Personality Tree* (London: Word Publishing, 1986), 14.
4. Larry Crabb, *Understanding People* (Grand Rapids: Zondervan Publishing House, 1987), 15.
5. Wayne W. Dyer, *The Power of Intention* (Carlsbad: Hay House, Inc., 2004), 26.
6. Ibid., 50.
7. Philip Yancey, *What's So Amazing About Grace?,* 56.
8. Chris Hedges, *Empire of Illusion* (New York: Nation Books, 2009), 193.

Chapter 16: Restoration of God's Boundary

1. James Strong, *The New Strong's Exhaustive Concordance of the Bible* (Nashville: Thomas Nelson Publishers, 1990).
2. Harold Kushner, *To Life!* (London: Little, Brown and Company, 1993), 51.

3. Henry Cloud and John Townsend, *Boundaries* (Grand Rapids: Zondervan Publishing House, 1992), 29.

Chapter 17: Fragrance of Grace

1. James Strong, *Strong's Exhaustive Concordance of the Bible* (Nashville: Thomas Nelson Publishers, 1990), 77.

Chapter 18: Man's Last Revolt Against the Creator

1. South by Southwest (SXSW) presentation, "The Holy Grail: Machine Learning and Extreme Robotics," March 13, 2016, Austin Convention Center, Austin, TX.
2. Yuval Noah Harari, *Sapiens: A Brief History of Humankind* (New York: HarperCollins Publishers, 2015), 403.
3. Ibid., 403–405.
4. Ibid., 404.
5. Ibid., 403.

Chapter 19: Thirsty for a Powerful World Leader

1. Bob Gundry, *First the Antichrist* (Grand Rapids: Baker House Books, 1997), 9.
2. Grant R. Jeffrey, *Messiah* (Toronto: Frontier Research Publication, 1991), 79.

Chapter 20: The Hope of Ultimate Restoration

1. W.E. Vine, *Expository Dictionary of Old and New Testament Words*, F. F. Bruce, ed. (New Jersey: Fleming H. Revell Company, 1981).

Chapter 22: Final Reflections

1. Sweet, 35.
2. John A. Sanford, *The Kingdom Within*, rev. ed. (New York: HarperOne, 1987), 45.
3. D. M. Lloyd-Jones, *Romans* (Grand Rapids: Zondervan Publishing House, 1985), 55.

Contact Information

To order additional copies of this book, please visit
www.redemption-press.com.
Also available on Amazon.com and BarnesandNoble.com
Or by calling toll free 1-844-2REDEEM.